Collecting
Chinese Export
Porcelain

Collecting Chinese Export Porcelain

Elinor Gordon

Foreword by J. A. Lloyd Hyde

John Murray

First published in Great Britain 1978
by John Murray, Albemarle Street, London

Copyright © 1977 by Elinor Gordon
All Rights Reserved

Designed by Robert Cihi
Color photographs by Helga Photo Studio

Printed in the United States of America
SBN 0 7195 3460 7

Contents

Foreword

The remarkable collection formed over a long period by Elinor and Horace Gordon covers in the most comprehensive way the whole fascinating spectrum of porcelain made in China solely for export to the West. The character of the ware has ever so many facets, each of which is reflected in this collection: it is beautiful in most respects; it is grotesque in others; it is humorous and it is sad; but, above all, it is history depicted on porcelain, and history that has a very long story indeed. Chinaware made for export was produced from sometime in the sixteenth century of the Western calendar until virtually the beginning of the twentieth century—four-hundred long and full years.

This porcelain has intrigued me for over half a century. I believe it must be the most fascinating of all the arts to collect. Its variety is infinite—never ending. The china is as delightful to the eye as it is to the touch. It has little of the fragility of glass, prints, paintings, fabrics, old books, or other categories. This helps to explain why so very much of it is still extant, given the normal accidents which are bound to happen. Among the man-made arts, only objects in marble, bronze, silver, gold, or precious stones have survived the centuries better. The finest of the export ware—the so-called "eggshell" porcelain—is not strong, of course; but one can say that nine-tenths of the porcelains made for shipment to the West are durable and rather heavy.

Elinor and Horace Gordon fell in love with this china and all its romantic story even as I did. Otherwise they would never have gone to such infinite pains and great expense to pursue it to the ends of the earth, for a diverse and fine collection of Chinese export porcelain, alas, is not to be had for a pittance. The Gordons have concentrated on wares of the seventeenth and eighteenth centuries which are increasingly hard to find. Prices for such rare pieces have risen over the years accordingly. The Gordon collection is especially rich in British and continental European armorial examples. Most of these can be dated, and all are of high quality. The various objects from the van Goudriaan service (color plate II) are extremely fine.

Porcelains with European scenes are exceptionally well represented in this collection. I find the plate with the two Scottish regimental soldiers, figure 58, a very charming piece. The figures are well rendered in every respect. A curious and intriguing example of the wedding of Chinese artistry with European subject matter is the dinner plate, figure 59, with two golfing scenes taken from European engravings. This is an example that I have never heard of, much less seen, and although the design is poorly executed, it is in every respect unique.

The Gordon collection is also especially rich in examples made for the American market, beginning with those bearing the seal of The Society of the Cincinnati. Some of these objects belonged to General Washington. All were made after 1784 when the first American consulate anywhere in the world was established by Major Samuel Shaw at Canton on the Pearl River. Views of American ships, often those from Salem; pieces with the arms of the new-born United States or the arms of the states of New York and New Hampshire; and a variety of pieces in the so-called "Fitzhugh" pattern, always popular on this side of the Atlantic, help to document the history of both China and the United States. The Gordons have carefully collected rare armorial pieces made for families living in America, and simpler wares bearing not arms, but more democratic motifs—even the homely cow!

No reader of this book should pass over the delightful and beguiling collection of animal figures. The Gordons have only reluctantly parted with them from time to time for exhibition. The deer figure made in underglaze blue for the Dutch market, c. 1720 (color plate XIII), is a great rarity and has been exhibited at the Metropolitan Museum of Art. Especially charming is the pair of iron-red hound figures dating from the mid-eighteenth century (color plate XIV). They seem almost to be grinning at the observer.

The Chinese artisans called their fine export porcelains "vases of the sea." The beauty and romance with which they are imbued will endure for many more centuries. With proper study and understanding, the collector can enrich immeasurably his own appreciation of the value and merits of these porcelains. *Collecting Chinese Export Porcelain* is a most useful aid to that worthwhile end.

J. A. Lloyd Hyde
Newport, Rhode Island
June, 1977

Acknowledgments

The writing of any book on collecting can never be a solitary pursuit. Reference is made in the text to a number of persons who have made their expert knowledge and skills available to me in the preparation of *Collecting Chinese Export Porcelain*. My particular thanks are due to five friends who have devoted an unusual amount of time and energy to this project: my husband, Horace, whose encouragement has been steadfast since our early collecting days; Lawrence Grow, my editor, without whose patient help this book would not be possible; J. A. Lloyd Hyde, my teacher and friend who always has been willing to answer my questions and share his special knowledge; and to Ellen and Bertram Denker who undertook the complex task of documenting each object included in these pages.

Preparation of an exhibition based on the book has been in the capable hands of Cathryn McElroy, Curator of Decorative Arts of the William Penn Memorial Museum. Special thanks are also owed to the following museum staff members: James Mitchell, Director; Gail Getz, Assistant Curator of Decoration Arts; Terrence Musgrave, Staff Photographer; and Peter C. Welsh, Director of the Bureau of Museums, Commonwealth of Pennsylvania.

Other persons and institutions who have offered special assistance over the years that has proved invaluable are Charles Hummel, The Henry Francis du Pont Winterthur Museum; J. Jefferson Miller, Museum of History and Technology, Smithsonian Institution; John Goldsmith Phillips and Clare Le Corbeiller, Metropolitan Museum; John Aures, Victoria and Albert Museum; Clement E. Conger, Chairman, Fine Arts Committee of the Department of State and Curator of the White House; H. A. Crosby Forbes and Paul E. Molitor, Jr., Museum of the American China Trade; Theodore Hayes, David Newborn, David Sanctuary Howard, Aaron Aronson, Earle van Deker, Theodore Beckhardt, the Dietrich Brothers Americana Foundation, the Henry Francis du Pont Winterthur Museum Libraries, the Rijksmuseum, Amsterdam, Holland, and the Göteborg Museum, Sweden.

For their role in making this book such an attractive volume, I wish to thank Robert Cihi, designer, and Arthur Vitols of Helga Studios who supplied the color photographs.

Elinor Gordon
August 15, 1977

Note to the reader: The following abbreviations appear in the illustration captions for the sake of brevity—
Diam = diameter
OH = overall height
OL = overall length
OW = overall width

Introduction

The widespread interest in Chinese export porcelain today reflects a new appreciation of the fine art of the Oriental craftsman. Potters and decorators in Ching-tê Chên, Canton, and Tê-Hua knew only that they were producing commercial wares for Western customers. The finest of these, the armorial services and the *blanc de chine* figures, were then and still are considered *objets d'art*; the vast bulk of the ware shipped to the West from the sixteenth through the early years of the nineteenth centuries was of a functional sort. While they were highly admired for their decorative qualities, these many forms were shaped for practical use. That one could impress guests with the beauty of a table setting was surely not a minor consideration of the buyer, but he was purchasing something for the home and not a museum. Only in recent times have these relatively late porcelains found their way into great private and public collections. Now, if one were to suggest dining off of a fine mid-eighteenth century *famille rose* service, guests would find it difficult to bring themselves to eat. Chinese export porcelain has become the province of the collector and the curator, and its monetary value has also greatly appreciated. The pursuit of such justly acclaimed objects requires specific expertise. It also calls for a special understanding of historical usage and development, a perspective which places the porcelain in a meaningful and not artificial context. *Collecting Chinese Export Porcelain* attempts to meet these needs in a simple and direct fashion.

This volume is based on a collection assembled over a thirty-five-year period. It is by no means definitive but it is representative of export production from the late 1600s to the early 1800s, the most important years in which wares were manufactured specifically for foreign customers. The commentary throughout the text is based primarily on three hundred and fifty objects which are currently on public exhibit; of these, approximately two hundred are illustrated in this volume. Thousands of such pieces have passed through this writer's hands during a long career as a dealer, and these have extended our knowledge immeasurably. Unfortunately, it is not possible to possess them all. Indeed, it has often been difficult to follow the sound advice once offered by the late Israel Sack—"Try to keep for yourself about one out of every ten pieces."

Every collector knows the search for fine antique objects can assume maniacal proportions. It is perhaps fortunate, then, that economic necessity has forced one to pass on to others duplicates, pairs, some priceless one-of-a-kind items, as well as those objects which, while outstanding in every respect, do not evoke a positive aesthetic response. Collecting is, above all, a subjective, personal matter and no one can live for long with objects that do not please him. Nonetheless, it is necessary to abide by as many of the objective rules of judging and selecting antiques as is possible. Paramount among these strictures is the rule of quality. Mistakes have been made (and, doubtless, will occur in the future), but every attempt has been made to buy only the best example of a particular style or form. The second-rate, despite the passage of time, will never be more than just that. How one goes about selecting the quality object is a question that can not be easily answered. It is a skill that can be gained only with experience, through trial and error. Hopefully, this volume will help in a small way to avoid some of these increasingly costly errors.

In this endeavor we have depended greatly on the work of others, fellow collectors and dealers, researchers, and writers. Throughout the book a number of key reference works are cited. They have saved us many hours of work and an unknown number of missteps. As armorial porcelain has been one of our principal interests, the work of David Sanctuary Howard has been indispensable. And, most fortunately, he has become our good friend. His comprehensive volume, *Chinese Armorial Porcelain*, is a constant companion, and is highly recommended to anyone seriously committed to the pursuit of these aristocratic wares. Researchers and writers from the Henry Francis du Pont Winterthur Museum and the Museum of the American China Trade have provided useful insights and specific assistance. The works of such accomplished historians as D. F. Lunsingh Scheurleer, John Goldsmith Phillips, Michel Beurdeley, and Clare Le Corbeiller are always informative and a pleasure to read. This writer's only regret is not having had the opportunity to talk with Homer Eaton Keyes, the former editor of *Antiques* who died prematurely in the 1930s. His witty and sophisticated writings on export ware have been gathered in an anthology of *Antiques*'s material, *Chinese Export Porcelain*, which this author was privileged to compile for book publication.

Every field of collecting has its special language and just a cursory look at any of the works cited above will confirm this fact. Experts do not always agree on either terms or their definitions, but there is a general understanding that can be conveyed. For years, of course, Chinese export porcelain was termed "Oriental Lowestoft," an unfortunate mistake in identification which still resists extinction. The term "Chinese export porcelain" is itself of recent vintage; in the past it has been variously called "China trade porcelain" or "Chinese trade porcelain." Export seems to be a more precise term, at least for the time being, as it allows for those objects which were made for export but were not necessarily carried by merchants involved in the historic European and North American China trade. Decorative styles used at various times are usually labelled by such terms as *famille rose, famille verte, blanc de chine, encre de chine* or *grisaille*, Imari, Jesuit, Fitzhugh, and *bianco sopra bianco*, to name the principal ones. Collectors of nineteenth-century wares, especially those made for the American market, are involved with yet another set of labels—Rose Medallion, Canton, Nanking, Mandarin. Generally, we have not collected such wares, and their story is not part of this volume. Many excellent objects of this later period were manufactured, and these are currently coming to the fore.

The various earlier styles and forms are illustrated and explained in a text divided into thirteen sections. The vast majority of the objects were made for the European market, and of these, most are decorated in the *famille rose* palette of opaque enamel colors. Such colors were the first "soft" shades to be used and were introduced in the reign of Yung Chêng, 1723–1735. Those termed "hard" by the Chinese, the *famille verte*, are of a translucent blue sort and are further divided into *famille jaune* and *famille noire* categories according to the background color. These were used during the K'ang Hsi period (1662–1722) and infrequently thereafter. Also important during this very early time are the blue and white porcelains employing only an underglaze blue, and the Chinese Imari wares based on a Japanese decorative style which combines underglaze blue and over the glaze *rouge de fer* or iron-red and gold. *Blanc de chine* refers to the finely glazed white porcelain of Tê-Hua in the Fukien province, primarily modeled figures without extensive decoration in color. *Bianco sopra bianco* is an Italian term used to describe a decorative design etched in opaque white on a pale bluish or greyish white ground, and this technique was mastered by the Chinese in the mid-1700s. Jesuit and Fitzhugh are less precise labels which fit very loosely. Simply, Jesuit refers to those objects with European religious and/or mythological scenes which are thought to have been inspired by Jesuit missionaries in residence in Ching-tê Chên; these are described more extensively in section IV. For a definition of the curious term "Fitzhugh," the reader is advised to turn to section IX. The development of this utterly imprecise label is a story that is still unraveling. *Encre de chine* describes a method of painting in black which the Chinese porcelain painters perfected in their copying of European engravings in the early 1700s. This has often been referred to as decoration in *grisaille,* but the suitability of using this French decorative term has been questioned in recent years. Similarly, a reddish-brown color found on much eighteenth-century ware is referred to as both iron-red and *rouge de fer.*

Covered custard cup, 1790–1810, American or English market. OH: 3¼" (8.2 cm), OW: 3½" (8.9 cm).

Numerous patterns are commonly acknowledged in all literature. For the most part, we have avoided them whenever possible. The variations or exceptions to these are encountered almost as often as the exemplars themselves. The special terminology applied to various border designs is a great deal more useful and accurate. Of these, the several forms of diapering (to weave or decorate in a diamond, Y, or cell-shape) are most often found on eighteenth-century porcelains. Other common border designs are those of the spearhead, reminiscent of the fleur-de-lis form; simple chain; Greek key or meander; *laub-und-bandelwerk*, a leaf and strapwork pattern copied from Meissen ware; and grape and vine. As seen in the illustration, customers could choose a particular border design or combination thereof. The buyer in Canton would leave specific instructions for the painting of the central design and select a border pattern from among those shown on various sample pieces. This covered custard cup was at some time brought to America; a similar object, also with the monogram "AT", is in the collection of the Henry Francis du Pont Winterthur Museum.

A basic knowledge of forms and decorative styles and techniques, the essentials of the porcelain trade, is indispensable, but it must be accompanied by a deeper understanding of motifs and their meaning. The forms from which one can choose are almost inexhaustible; the Chinese were fairly proficient in copying whatever was brought to them via wooden or metal models, sketches, or actual pieces of European-made ware. Proficient, yes, but objects were not always inspired or even pleasing copies. Crudities exist in this field as they do in every other area of antiques. The first dinner services contained every imaginable kind of object; by the mid-eighteenth century the number had been greatly reduced. Yet, the collector can examine a rich variety of dishes, figures, and assorted objects in public collections throughout the world. Among the most important in America are those of the Metropolitan Museum of Art; Peabody Museum; Winterthur Museum; Philadelphia Museum of Art; Museum of Fine Arts in Boston; and the Museum of the American China Trade, in Milton, Massachusetts; the British Museum and the Victoria and Albert Museum in London; the Musée Guimet in Paris; the Museu Nacional de Arte Antiga and the Espirito Santo Foundation, Lisbon; and Rijksmuseum, Amsterdam; and Geemeente Museum, Leeuwarden, Holland.

The Helena Woolworth McCann collection of approximately 4,000 pieces of export ware was given to the Winfield Foundation in 1938. These objects were in turn dispersed to twenty-seven American and Canadian museums. In addition to the already-mentioned American museums, the following institutions display a considerable number of pieces which the collector will find of special interest: Brooklyn Museum; Albright-Knox Art Gallery, Buffalo; Art Institute of Chicago; Cincinnati Art Museum; Cleveland Museum of Art; Dallas Museum of Fine Arts; Detroit Institute of Arts; Monmouth County Historical Association, Freehold, New Jersey; Beauport, Gloucester, Massachusetts; Wadsworth Atheneum, Hartford, Connecticut; Museum of Fine Arts of Houston; William Rockhill Nelson Gallery of Art, Kansas City,

Missouri; Los Angeles County Museum; J. B. Speed Art Museum, Louisville, Kentucky; Minneapolis Institute of Arts; Norfolk Museum of Arts and Sciences, Norfolk, Virginia; Joslyn Memorial Art Museum, Omaha, Nebraska; Portland Art Museum, Portland, Oregon; Museum of Art, Rhode Island School of Design, Providence; Virginia Museum of Fine Arts, Richmond; City Art Museum of St. Louis; M. H. DeYoung Memorial Museum, San Francisco; Springfield Museum of Fine Arts, Springfield, Massachusetts; Toledo Museum of Art; and Royal Ontario Museum of Archaeology, Toronto, Canada.

The collector must look for the best pieces, and examine them for those traits which define their quality. Glazes should adhere closely to the body; colors ought to be vibrant and evenly applied; lines carefully and expertly drawn; forms gracefully and accurately modeled. An appropriateness of color combinations and decorative style will emerge through such careful viewing. An armorial plate of the sort illustrated here from the K'ang Hsi period, will

Plate, K'ang Hsi,
c. 1720, English
market. Diam: 8⅞″
(22.6 cm).

likely display a Chinese border design rather than a European one. The reverse of the rim may contain four *rouge-de-fer* flowers, a practice discontinued after 1725. These are present on this plate displaying the arms of Heathcote impaling Parker and quartering Venables and Carrier. On a later amorial piece, however, the coat of arms may have been moved to the border from the center. The second armorial plate displays the arms of a branch of Gordon, quarterly, quartering Forbes, in the border.

Octagonal plate, Ch'ien Lung, c. 1745, English market.
OH: $^{15}\!/_{16}''$ (2.4 cm), Diam: $8^{3}\!/_{8}''$ (21.4 cm).

When turning to objects with floral, religious, mythological, or genre designs, a different set of credentials will emerge. The barber's basin is typical of the *famille rose* floral wares and exhibits a delicacy of line and coloring which is hardly to be matched by even French porcelains of the same period.

Barber basin, Ch'ien Lung, c. 1740, European market.
$13^{3}\!/_{4}''$ (35 cm) x 11″ (27.9 cm).

The plate displaying two roosters is decorated entirely in underglaze blue. This method of decoration, most popular in the early 1700s, continued to be used throughout the century. The flower and leaf border is confirmation of a mid-century date, a time confirmed by documentation in records of the Swedish East India Company. The very baroque border design of the "Diana at the bath" plate fixes it in time as mid-century. Further research indicates that the scene itself is an adaptation from the *Metamorphoses* of Ovid drawn from engravings popular since the seventeenth century. The border design

Plate, Ch'ien Lung, c. 1745, Swedish market. Diam: 9″ (22.9 cm).

Plate, Ch'ien Lung, c. 1745, European market. Diam: $8^{15}/_{16}$″ (22.8 cm).

of the plate showing a portrait of Martin Luther and Christ and his disciples can also be ascribed to the mid-eighteenth century. The subject matter suggests that not all porcelain with religious symbolism was Jesuit-inspired; indeed, the Protestant Dutch and English traders were similarly active in China. The special role of the merchants of the Dutch East Indies Company is conveyed on numerous pieces of export ware. The plate showing a view of the Nieuwe Stadsherberg (New Town Inn) on a wharf in Amsterdam was duplicated many times throughout the 1700s; the simple border with floral sprigs indicates that the piece is a late one. An even more classic, chaste border design is found in the "Maid of Spring" plate. The figure is taken from a larger print by Larmessin after a drawing by Lancret, "Le Printemps."

Plate, Ch'ien Lung, c. 1740, European market. Diam: 8⅞″ (22.6 cm).

Plate, Ch'ien Lung, c. 1770, Dutch market. Diam: 9″ (22.9 cm).

Plate, Ch'ien Lung, c. 1750, European market. Diam: 9" (22.9 cm).

Figures of rooster and hen, Ch'ien Lung, c. 1750–75, European market. OH (rooster): 5%₁₆" (14.2 cm), OL: 6" (15.2 cm); OH (hen): 3⅞" (9.8 cm), OL: 5⅛" (13 cm).

Figures of animal forms are much more difficult to date. These of a rooster and hen were probably copied from European models and are very realistically painted. The manufacture of such items was a much more speculative affair than that of dinner services or tea sets. These are novelties, knick-knacks of the time, which were most often reproduced in response to specific demands for particular European forms. Until late in the eighteenth century, such figures could be purchased at a lower price than comparable objects from Meissen, Sèvres, Worcester, etc. *Blanc de chine* figures are considerably more rare, and in this case the Europeans copied the Chinese rather than vice versa.

Porcelain made specifically for the American market is less varied in form and decoration, and, of course, dates from a later period. The strange story of the "Fitzhugh" pattern is traced elsewhere, and it is an important one. The central medallion and four floral panels are represented in the rectangular dish. The border, a composition of birds, floral sprays, and butterflies, is an unusual feature. A more traditional "Fitzhugh" border is seen in the plate from George Washington's Society of the Cincinnati service. One of the most rare of American-market porcelains, this plate carries a single figure of Fame holding a ribbon from which is suspended the Society's insignia, a story which is told more completely in section X. Another exclusively American piece is that carrying an adaptation of the arms of New York. The naïve representation of the figures on this pseudo-armorial plate does not detract from its historical value. Plates of this sort often have been copied by forgers. But in their greed for a fast and easy dollar, they most often do *too* fine a job with the figures, rendering them with much more finesse than is necessary.

Rectangular dish, Chia Ch'ing, c. 1800, American market, 8⅛″ (20.7 cm) x 6¾″ (17.1 cm).

Plate, Ch'ien Lung, c. 1784–85, American market. Diam: 9½″ (24.2 cm).

Plate, Ch'ien Lung, c. 1790, American market. Diam: 7⅝″ (19.4 cm).

The next two photographs in this section illustrate two of the most common motifs found on American-market ware—the ship bearing the stars and stripes and the bald eagle. It should be noted that very similar ship designs also appear on mugs intended for the British market. The eagle, or "sparrow" so-called by Homer Eaton Keyes, is as rendered a uniquely Chinese creation. Modern-day forgers of such rare objects often fail to approximate the primitive lines of these first porcelain eagles, or if they are successful in restraining their artistic impulses, they sometimes place the eagle on a plate with a border totally untrue to this time and type of decoration. A pink *famille rose* border, as was found on one recent fake, was just not the appropriate one!

Bowl, Chia Ch'ing, c. 1800, American market. OH: 1⅜" (3.5 cm), Diam: 7¾" (19.7 cm).

Cylindrical mug, Ch'ien Lung, c. 1790, American market. OH: 4⅜" (11.2 cm).

Collectors must always be aware of such forgeries. The relatively simple American-market wares are copied most frequently as it is possible to alter or remove a central decorative motif and replace it with a more valuable Cincinnati emblem, or the arms of New York State. If there is any question about the authenticity of an object, it should be held up to a light and examined for a rubbed area in the center. An altered piece will display a dullness in the center where the new decoration has been added. Marks, unfortunately, are of no help for they rarely exist. A few early eighteenth-century porcelains may display the reign mark of K'ang Hsi, but since use of this mark or that of any subsequent reign was forbidden on export ware, its presence may be more a cause for alarm than its absence.

Export ware redecorated in Europe is known in Great Britain and the United States as "clobbered" ware. Pieces of this sort were produced as early as the late sixteenth century and should not be confused with the fakes being made today. Indeed, as Scheurleer has commented, "there are specimens which have a certain rustic charm of their own." Porcelain blanks were imported by the English and Dutch for decoration by local artists. As well, sparsely embellished objects such as those in underglaze blue were redecorated or added to. Quite often these additions obscured the original decoration, hence the term "clobbered." On the cream jug illustrated here the Chinese underglaze blue decoration has been almost entirely covered by a lime-colored glaze; the flowers in red and gold follow the lines of the underglaze blue flowers over which they have been painted.

Side-handled cream jug, Ch'ien Lung, c. 1770, European market. OH: 4⁷⁄₁₆″ (11.3 cm).

All of this is not said to dampen the enthusiasm of a new collector for one of the most colorful and pleasurable of antiquarian pastimes. Although the prices of quality wares are rising rapidly, there is a quite sufficient stock of porcelains available to be discovered. As noted in section I on armorial porcelains, 60,000,000 objects were shipped to Europe in the eighteenth century alone! The early *famille verte* and underglaze blue objects of the seventeenth and early eighteenth centuries are now the province of the museum curator. Fine pieces in *famille rose* decoration in every conceivable form are offered in the world's antiques markets each day of the year. These may be of the fine eggshell variety or slightly heavier wares of an armorial sort. Blue "Fitzhugh" pieces are also widely available in numerous forms and are modest in price compared with the same pattern in orange, green, or other colors. In time, this blue ware will rise to a corresponding level of value.

Chinese export porcelains are true hard paste objects. The hard, glazed surface cannot be scratched by a steel knife and it will not absorb liquids or acids. If broken, it will display a grainy construction rather than the smooth edge found on soft paste wares. If struck, this porcelain gives off a very resonant ring. The glaze itself is slightly blue in color, and has a somewhat uneven surface called by one expert the "musliny" appearance of orange peel. The enamel color gives the appearance of subtly blending into the glaze. Such attributes as these represent the distinctions, the nuances of a particular antique art form which one absorbs with time. To discover those special objects which "ring true" in every respect is an exciting experience. Looking back on a past filled with such pleasurable moments, there is no doubt that they are hard earned but well worth searching out. If only one could live them over again, but then these pleasures of the past, both personal and antique, can only be passed on for rediscovery, and that is the way it should be.

Collecting
Chinese Export
Porcelain

I. British and Continental European Armorial Services

Armorial porcelains from China are the true treasures of the historic trade between East and West which began with the Portuguese in the sixteenth century and reached a peak with the Americans in the first decades of the nineteenth century. These are the finest executed objects to emerge from what was a purely commercial venture, the manufacturing and distribution of massive amounts of domestic china at a cost lower than that obtainable in Europe. Even the most sophisticated critic of the purely decorative object must agree with the assessment of Homer Eaton Keyes, *Antiques* magazine's first and most hard-to-please editor, rendered some thirty-seven years ago: "The Chinese makers appear to have lavished more intelligent and painstaking effort on their armorial services than upon any other of their foreign-market porcelains. Many surviving examples of the type display really exquisite workmanship, combined with an impeccable balance of design."[1]

As noted by many experts, it has been estimated that at least 60,000,000 pieces of porcelain were shipped to the West in the 1700s alone. Objects with armorial decoration account for only 1% of this total. Some 5,000 dinner and tea services of the armorial type are known to have been sent to Europe, and of these, 4,000 were intended for the British market. Only a few such services were ordered from and for North America. The typical armorial object cost ten times more than a common piece then, and nearly this same scale of values applies today. Armorial porcelains were not stocked by the Canton merchants for everyday sale; they were special order items that might take as many as two years to complete. In at least the first half of the eighteenth century all were produced and decorated at Ching-tê Chên.[2] Louis XIV ordered a Chinese dinner service of 1,058 pieces; other individuals of less lofty station routinely requested sets of two to three hundred pieces. The Chinese were prepared to handle such orders. For several hundred years the potters and painters of Ching-tê Chên had produced an enormous number of objects for the Imperial court and for other domestic usages. When aristocratic Europe turned to porcelain from silver for their table settings in the first quarter of the eighteenth century, the Chinese were delighted to oblige them. In addition, the drinking of tea had been introduced in Europe during the mid-seventeenth century and as Dutch historian D. F. Lunsingh Scheurleer has explained, "people wanted a tea service the component parts of which were matching in decoration and harmonious in shape."[3] They could, of course, turn to the Delft potters of England and Holland for their wares, and many did, but the more selective of customers wanted only the Chinese in the same way that today a connoisseur of fine brocades and silks will turn only to Italian suppliers.

It should not surprise us to find that a vast majority of the fine armorial wares were sent to the British Isles. Members of England's fast growing merchant class of the eighteenth century, including many members of the

British East Indies Company, were among the first to want porcelain emblazoned with the identifying emblem of their upwardly mobile family. They were, of course, joined in this desire by their more aristocratic peers with heraldic shields that may have been quartered among as many as eight or ten families. Only the Dutch were as avid in their acquisition of fine Chinese armorial porcelain.

The manufacture and trade in armorial porcelain requires, and is worthy of, voluminous single volumes, and these, fortunately, do exist. David Sanctuary Howard's *Chinese Armorial Porcelain* is an indispensable guide to this complex subject.[4] All collectors are indebted to his keen judgment and practiced eye. The documentation of all of the objects illustrated here, as well as many others not included, would have been impossible without his assistance. Readers also can turn to Sir Algernon Tudor-Craig's early work or, if they are especially industrious, refer to some of the basic handbooks on heraldry and peerage for help in identifying family arms. An elementary knowledge of heraldry is a must for any serious collector of armorial ware. The rules are complex but once mastered they will prove of great benefit. Suffice to say, these complicated matters can not be outlined here in any detail. Simply, a coat of arms is made up of a shield for a man and a diamond-shaped lozenge for a woman. A small shield placed within a larger one, however, may take the place of the lozenge in the arms of a married heiress or co-heiress. Other elements that may be included in the coat of arms are a helmet, a crest supported by a wreath, an ornamental drapery termed a mantle or lambrequin, and a motto which often appears on a scroll placed under the shield and, if granted, supporters on each side of the shield. The divisions within the shield itself are of considerable importance:

> In the case of a husband and wife both entitled to take arms the shield may be divided vertically or impaled, with the husband's arms on the left and the wife's on the right. Their son might then divide the escutcheon into four quarters, with his father's arms on the upper right and lower left and his mother's in the other two sections. This quartering might continue to be sub-divided so that coats of arms sometimes becomes very complex.[5]

Complex, indeed! Turn to Howard as we have. The Chinese must have been just as mystified as modern man by such symbolic accoutrements. It is known that they relied on bookplates and sketches to copy the arms. The early services, however, were basically Oriental in those design elements outside of the center area. Most of the first services were decorated in underglaze blue and/or *famille verte* colors. The Talbot platter, figure 1, is illustrative of such a rare object. Nearly as rare as this is the Duke of Chandos charger, color plate IV, which displays the Chinese Imari style in underglaze blue, *rouge de fer*, and gilt. Much more typical of armorial ware in general are those objects in *famille rose* colors introduced during the 1730s. Of these, the earliest were surely produced in their entirety at Ching-tê Chên. They give great play to the central coat-of-arms. But by the 1750s the size of this decorative element was gradually to be reduced; eventually the arms were often placed in the border. Border designs can be used as a means of dating various armorial services, the earliest from the K'ang Hsi period employing such traditional Chinese symbols as the "Eight Precious Objects" and the latest, of the 1780s on, often displaying the "Fitzhugh" pattern.

Of all the various types of armorial porcelains (Howard lists twenty-four basic styles and breaks these down into 236 sub-divisions), those of a familial sort are by far the most common. Collectors, however, should also be aware of objects made for private societies, public bodies, and companies such as the European trading organizations. The Bucks punch bowl, color plate I, is a particularly rare example of this latter type, and was made for a fashionable, private social organization in Liverpool. Objects commissioned by other groups are illustrated in figures 5, 24, and 26.

The very personal possessions of historically-important families have for us the most direct appeal and interest. One needs only to study such beautiful objects as those produced for the van Goudriaan family, color plate II, the van Reverhorsts, figure 12, von Herzeele, figure 3, and Okeover, figure 13, to recognize that the potters and decorators of the China trade were, at their best, not only craftsmen but fine artists. These were porcelains that were prized for many years by their original owners. The fifty plates and four large dishes ordered by Leake Okeover in the early 1740s remained with members of the family until fairly recently. Still possessed by them is the original drawing—"a pattern for china plate"—taken to China for copying and then returned.[6]

NOTES

[1] Homer Eaton Keyes, "Centres of Manufacture and a Classification," *Chinese Export Porcelain*, ed. Elinor Gordon (New York: Universe Books, 1975), p. 26.

[2] When the decoration of armorial wares began in Canton and to what extent this practice flourished there is very much a matter of controversy among the several authorities in the field.

[3] D. F. Lunsingh Scheurleer, *Chinese Export Porcelain* (London: Faber and Faber, Ltd., 1974 and New York: Pitman Publishing Corp., 1974), p. 102.

[4] David Sanctuary Howard, *Chinese Armorial Porcelain* (London: Faber and Faber, Ltd., 1974).

[5] Jane Boicourt, "Introduction to Heraldry," *Chinese Export Porcelain*, ed. Elinor Gordon (New York: Universe Books, 1975), p. 150.

[6] A. Oswald, "Okeover Hall—Staffordshire II," *Country Life* (30 January, 1964), p. 228.

1   Octagonal platter, K'ang Hsi, c. 1705, English
market. One of the earliest armorial services
made for an English family bears the arms of
TALBOT. All in underglaze blue, the coat of arms
is in the center with a wide decorative border
representing the Chinese arts and some of the
pa pao ("Eight Precious Objects"). There are
four floral sprigs on the reverse of the rim in
underglaze blue. The Right Reverend William
Talbot served consecutively as Dean of Worcester (1691), Bishop of Oxford (1699), Bishop
of Salisbury (1715), and Bishop of Durham
(1722). The Talbot arms which are borne by
the earls of Shrewsbury feature a dog for the
crest; talbot is a variety of hound once used for
hunting. *See* Howard, pg. 164. 20½" (52.2 cm)
x 15" (38.1 cm).

2

Plate, Yung Chêng, c. 1723, English market. A more elaborate and less Oriental piece in decoration, the plate is part of a service made for Robert Wynne of Garthewin who married Diana Gosling. The arms are those of WYNNE of Garthewin impaling GOSLING, and are rendered in gilt, black, *rouge de fer*, and blue enamel colors. Four *rouge de fer* flowers are found on the reverse of the rim. This form of decoration generally disappears after 1725. Diam: 8¾″ (22.3 cm).

Plate, Yung Chêng, c. 1724, English market. The arms of FREDERICK with MARESCOE in pretence and impaling MARESCOE are emblazoned in polychrome enamels with gilt and *rouge de fer* decoration. The service was made for Leonora, widow of Thomas Frederick of Westminister, who died in June, 1720. The arms are displayed in a lozenge rather than a shield because a woman only bore arms when she was an "heraldic heiress" (no surviving males in the family were entitled to bear the family arms). The inner border of the plate is decorated in gilt; the outer is in blue, green, *rouge de fer*, and gilt. Diam: 8¹³⁄₁₆″ (22.5 cm).

4

Plate, Yung Chêng, c. 1725, Dutch market. A manager of the Dutch East India Company, Baron J. von Herzeele, ordered a service decorated with the VON HERZEELE arms. The coat is rendered in *rouge de fer*, and white, yellow, and blue enamel colors with gilt on a ground in *bianco-sopra-bianco*. The borders are in gilt with *encre de chine* and *rouge de fer* decoration. The service from which this piece comes is considered one of the most outstanding in export ware. *See* Scheurleer, pl. 270. Diam: 9" (22.9 cm).

3

Plate, Yung Chêng, c. 1725, Dutch market. The Dutch East India Company (Vereenigde Oostindische Compagnie) made a practice of giving gifts of porcelain to members of the government and magistrates at The Hague for certain trade considerations. This plate may have served such a purpose and carries the arms of THE HAGUE. It is brilliantly enameled with the arms in a blue lozenge enclosed by *rouge de fer* and yellow mantling below a coronet tied with *rouge de fer* ribbons. The branches are rendered in green, *rouge de fer*, and black. Other such plates were made with the arms of HOLLAND and the arms of the city of AMSTERDAM. *See* Beurdeley, pg. 92, fig. 64. Diam: 8³⁄₁₆" (20.9 cm).

5

Tankard, Yung Chêng, c. 1725, English market. The arms are those of BOOTHBY, quartering SCRIMSHIRE, and impaling CLOPTON of Warwick, and are drawn in rose, blue, *rouge de fer*, and gilt. On the reverse side is a Chinese vase holding flowers. Thomas Boothby of Norbury in Staffordshire assumed the name of Skrymshire and served as "Regulator General" of all ships trading with Britain. He married Anne, daughter of Sir Hugh Clopton, Bt. *See* Howard, pg. 203. OH: 9½" (24.2 cm) ; OW (including handles) : 7⅜" (27.4 cm) .

6

Plate, Yung Chêng, c. 1726, English market. Edward Alexander, who married Levina, daughter of Sir Levinus Bennet in the early eighteenth century, probably had this service made. The arms are those of ALEXANDER quartering BENNET, an unidentified family name, and EDMONDS. Both arms and the border are in gilt, *rouge de fer*, and black with blue enamel. Diam: 9" (22.9 cm) .

7

8

Plate, Yung Chêng, c. 1730, English market. The arms of HUSBANDS are found on the rim of this plate in polychrome enamel colors and gilt. The central floral decoration and borders are painted in gilt and *rouge de fer* with accents of blue enamel. The service was made for the Reverend James Husbands, LL.D., rector of Little Horkesley, Essex. Diam: 12¾″ (32.4 cm).

Plate, Yung Chêng, c. 1730, English market. The elaborate central arms are those of the IZOD family. Since they bear no crest and are arranged in a diamond-shaped shield (lozenge), it would seem the service from which this plate was taken was made for an unmarried daughter of an armigerous family, in this case, the daughter of Henry Izod. Various polychrome enamels and gilt are used in the decoration. This service is generally considered one of the most beautiful made. *See* Howard, pg. 237. Diam: 8¹¹⁄₁₆″ (22.2 cm).

9

Soup plate, Yung Chêng, c. 1735, English market. The arms found in the center of the plate belong to the Hanbury family and include the HANBURY crest with COMYN in pretence. The coat is drawn in gilt, *rouge de fer*, green, and black. The border is decorated with a gilt vine and a leaf scroll. The service was made for John Hanbury, a Quaker merchant in London, and was only recently broken up for sale. Pieces are still appearing in the American and British antiques markets. Diam: 8⅞" (22.6 cm).

10

Plate, Yung Chêng, c. 1735, English market. The arms of the same family may appear on several different services. This is the case here with HAGGARD, shown impaling LEE. According to David Howard, this service was probably made for John Haggard and his second wife, Elizabeth Lee. The arms are drawn in *encre de chine, rouge de fer,* polychrome enamels, and gilt; the borders are in gilt with *rouge de fer.* Diam: 9" (22.9 cm).

11

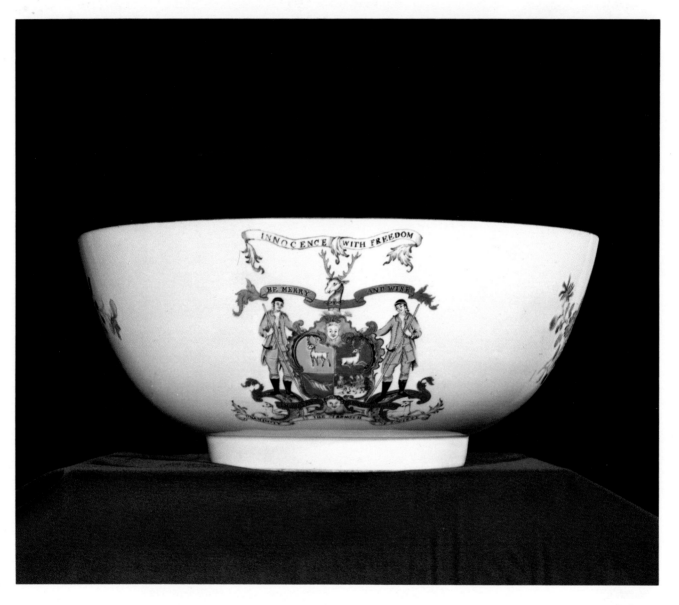

Plate I. Punch bowl, Ch'ien Lung, c. 1755, English market. The arms of THE SOCIETY OF BUCKS, an organization which flourished in Georgian England, emblazon this armorial piece. All decoration is in polychrome enamels and gilt. The banners display the mottoes INNOCENCE WITH FREEDOM, BE MERRY AND WISE, INDUSTRY PRODUCETH WEALTH, and UNANIMITY THE STRENGTH OF SOCIETY. The arms are those used by the society before 1757 when a new design was adopted. *See* Howard, pg. 452. OH: 4⅞″ (12.4 cm), Diam (top): 12⅛″ (30.8 cm).

Plate II.   From left to right, basket and underdish, large platter, punch pot and lid, covered tureen and stand, Ch'ien Lung, c. 1769, Dutch market. These objects are just a few from the large service made for Arnoldus Adrianus van Tets (1738–1792) and Wilhelmina Jacoba Hartingh (1750–1813) who married in 1767. The set descended to the van Goudriaan family of Rotterdam. The central arms are drawn in polychrome enamel colors—dark brown, black, gilt, and blue. Borders of the unpierced pieces are composed of gilt scrolled cartouches alternating with polychrome enamel floral sprays. Two of the cartouches contain cipher conceits while the others enclose figures in a landscape. Basket—10$\frac{3}{16}$" (25.9 cm) x 8$\frac{3}{16}$" (20.9 cm), OH: 4$\frac{1}{16}$" (10.3 cm). Underdish—11$\frac{5}{16}$" (28.7 cm) x 10$\frac{5}{16}$" (26.2 cm). Large platter—OL: 16$\frac{5}{8}$" (42.3 cm), OW: 13$\frac{3}{8}$" (34 cm). Punch pot and lid—OH: 7$\frac{1}{2}$" (19.1 cm). Covered tureen—13$\frac{1}{4}$" (33.7 cm) x 8$\frac{1}{2}$" (21.7 cm), OH: 8" (20.4 cm). Stand—14$\frac{7}{8}$" (37.8 cm) x 11$\frac{7}{8}$" (30.1 cm).

Plate III. Covered standing cup, Ch'ien Lung, c. 1780. English market. According to David Howard this piece is most probably from a service made for Captain Frederick LeMesurier of the East Indiaman "Ponsborne". The arms are those of LEMESURIER and the quartered coat is incorrect but painted for FITZLAY or ANDREWS, probably the latter. Polychrome enamel colors of sepia and gilt, lavender, and green are used to decorate the arms and crest. The cover and pedestal is gadrooned with lavender and green. Floral sprigs and swags are scattered over the piece. *See* Howard, pg. 628. OH: 13¾" (35 cm); OW: 10¼" (26 cm).

Plate IV. Charger, Yung Chêng, c. 1719 English market. James Brydges was advanced to the Dukedom of Chandos in 1718. In 1714 he had taken a second wife, Cassandra, daughter of Francis Willoughby and sister of Thomas, 1st. Lord Middleton. The large central arms are those of BRYDGES DUKE OF CHANDOS impaling WILLOUGHBY and MIDDLETON quarterly. The coronet is that of a duke and is surmounted by the Brydges crest and supporters. Arms, coronet, supporters, and banner below with motto "MAINTIEN LE DROIT" are drawn in *rouge-de-fer*, gilt, blue, and black. The wide floral border is composed of underglaze blue, *rouge-de-fer*, blue, and gilt. *See* Howard, pg. 181. Diam: 18½" (47 cm).

Plate V. Pitcher, Ch'ien Lung, c. 1755, English market. The arms of LYNCH are seen to the left in polychrome enamels. On either side are positioned landscapes with a rooster and hen amidst a delicate floral arrangement. The finely molded mask under the spout is decorated in *rouge de fer* with black details. The pitcher was made for the Very Reverend John Lynch, D.D., Dean of Canterbury, in the mid-eighteenth century. Dr. Lynch married Mary, daughter of the Most Reverend William Wake, D.D., Archbishop of Canterbury. The arms include, in pretence, those of WAKE quartering HOVELL. *See* Howard, pg. 402. OH: 13⅜″ (34 cm).

Sugar bowl, Ch'ien Lung, c. 1735–40. Dutch market. The covered sugar bowl with serpentine handles comes from one of the earliest Dutch armorial services and is a form apparently unique to the van Reverhorst family. The arms of VAN REVERHORST in red, blue, and green enamels are found in the center surrounded by the arms of Theodorus van Reverhorst's great-grandparents, SCHREVELIUS, VAN PEENE, VAN GROENENDYCK, DE VROEDE, VAN REVERHORST, DE WINTER, VEREYCK, and DE BRUYN. The service is reputed to have been ordered by van Reverhorst (1706–58), one-time Chief Justice at Batavia, Dutch East Indies, in memory of his father, Professor Doctor Mauritius van Reverhorst (1666–1722). OH: 4¾" (12.1 cm); Diam (top bowl): 4⅞" (12.4 cm).

12

Plate, Ch'ien Lung, c. 1743, English market. The arms of OKEOVER quarterly (with also BYRMINGHAM, PETTUS, and LEAKE) impaling NICHOL are found on this exceptional piece. The ciphers in the border, *MLO*, are for Mary and Leake Okeover. The original drawing of the Okeover arms is still in the possession of the family and is the only known survival of an armorial pattern actually sent to China for copying. The inscription on the drawing, perhaps executed by Arthur Davis in 1740, reads: "The Arms of Leake Okeover Esqre of Okeover near Ashbourn in the Peake in the County of Staffordshire—a pattern for china plate. Pattern to be returned." The complete Okeover service was recently sold at auction in England and the bill of sale that went with it indicates that the service is composed entirely of flat pieces such as plates, platters, etc.; no pitchers, tureens, covered dishes, etc., are included. Diam: 8⅜" (21.3 cm).

13

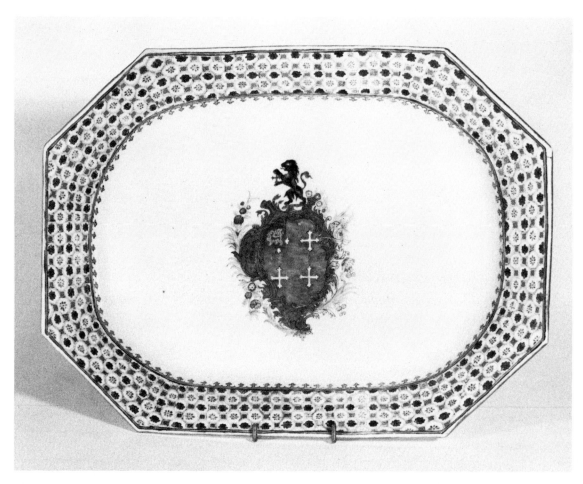

14

Octagonal platter, Ch'ien Lung, c. 1750, English market. This service was made for Sir Richard Chase, Sheriff of Essex in 1744, and contains the CHASE arms in *rouge de fer* and polychrome enamels. A distant American relative, Samuel Chase of Maryland, a signer of the Declaration of Independence, is sometimes thought to have used the same arms, but those he utilized belong to a Townley aunt. *See* Le Corbeiller, pg. 61. 13" (33 cm) x 9½" (24.2 cm).

15

Octagonal plate, Ch'ien Lung, c. 1755, English market. John Booth, the son of a wealthy merchant in the West Indies trade, had this service made after his marriage to Phoebe Wilkinson. Booth was the son of Anna Lloyd. The arms drawn in polychrome enamels with gilt and *rouge de fer* are those of BOOTH quartering LLOYD with WILKINSON in pretence. Diam: 8½" (21.7 cm).

16

Punch bowl, Ch'ien Lung, c. 1768, English market. A political rather
than heraldic message is carried on this distinctive piece. John Wilkes
is the hero and Lord Mansfield the culprit. To the left Wilkes is
shown, below a lion, with the motto "Always ready in a good cause";
at right Lord Mansfield, Lord Chief Justice from 1756–88 and the
pillar of the Establishment, is depicted below a serpent, with the
motto "Justice sans pitié" and two supporters, one being the devil.
Wilkes (1727–97) was a noted champion of personal liberty and the
American revolutionary cause. Other bowls with the inscription "Wilkes
and Liberty" carry the same design. *See* Howard, pg. 955. OH: 4⅜"
(11.1 cm); Diam (top): 10⅛" (25.1 cm).

Teapot, Ch'ien Lung, c. 1770, English market. Robert Clive, K.B., entered the service of the New East India Company in 1744 and in 1757 won his great victory at Plassey; in 1762 he was created Baron Clive of Plassey. This service was probably made for a brother or Lord Clive's father, Richard. The arms are those of CLIVE quartering six other families and surmounted by the Clive crest, and are drawn in *rouge de fer*, black, gilt, and blue enamel. OH: 6" (15.2 cm); OW (handle to spout): 9" (22.9 cm).

17

Platter, Ch'ien Lung, c. 1785, English market. Several services were made for the distinguished Caulfield family but this is a piece from a singular service; the decoration is done entirely in underglaze blue. The arms are those of CAULFIELD, 4th Viscount and 1st Earl of Charlemont. The outer border is decorated with the chain of the Order of St. Patrick (founded 1783). James Caulfield commanded the Volunteer Army in Ireland in 1779 and was a member of the honorary order. OW: 11½" (29.2 cm).

18

Oval platter, Ch'ien Lung, c. 1785–1800, Portuguese market. The arms are those of Bernardo Jose Maria de LORENA E SILVEIRA, fifth Count of Sarzedas, impaling TAVORA. He served as Portuguese viceroy in India during the late eighteenth century. The elaborate border motif of crossed branches is unusual and is derived from a Western prototype. OL: 6¾6″ (15.7 cm), OW: 4¹¹⁄₁₆″ (11.95 cm).

19

21

Bowl, Ch'ien Lung, c. 1790, English market. The arms of KER (CARR)-MARTIN are found in the central medallion and in the arms of the figure of Hope. The cartouches alternating with the arms show two of the four known quarters of the globe—Europe, represented by guns, merchandise, a cornucopia of plenty, and a lady brandishing symbols of peace and liberty; and America, by an Indian and a bison or bear and tobacco plants. Some other pieces in the service show all four quarters of the globe. The service was probably made for Jane, daughter of Ellis Martin and Elizabeth Ker, who married her first cousin, William Ker, c. 1790. Pieces from the Ker service are much sought after by collectors of armorial designs. *See* Howard, pg. 694. OH: 3¹⁵⁄₁₆″ (9.9 cm); Diam (top): 9″ (22.9 cm).

Bowl, Ch'ien Lung, c. 1790, English market. A naval coronet topped with five different types of sails is featured in the crest of the coat of arms belonging to Admiral Andrew Snape Hamond. Sir Andrew was knighted in 1778 after service in the Seven Years War and the American Revolutionary War. Green and black enamel colors are used to decorate the small central arms of HAMOND. The scenic and floral cartouches in the inner and outer borders are drawn in *rouge de fer*. OH: 2³⁄₁₆″ (5.6 cm); Diam: 11¹⁄₁₆″ (28.1 cm).

20

Plate, Ch'ien Lung, 1791, English market. A unique service, that of Chadwick, is the only one known to be dated on the reverse of each plate. The legend is "Canton/in China/24th Jany. 1791." The small central arms in *rouge de fer*, black, and gilt with green and purple enamel colors are those of CHADWICK quartering MALVESYN, CARDEN, and BAGOT. Larger pieces in the service such as platters show the arms with a quartering of six. The service was made for John Chadwick (1720–1800) and his wife, Susannah. Diam: 9⅞" (25.1 cm).

22

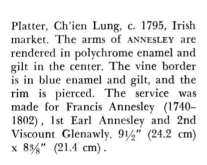

Platter, Ch'ien Lung, c. 1795, Irish market. The arms of ANNESLEY are rendered in polychrome enamel and gilt in the center. The vine border is in blue enamel and gilt, and the rim is pierced. The service was made for Francis Annesley (1740–1802), 1st Earl Annesley and 2nd Viscount Glenawly. 9½" (24.2 cm) x 8⅜" (21.4 cm).

23

24

Platter, Chia Ch'ing, c. 1800, British market. This service may have been made to commemorate the centenary of the incorporation of the NEW EAST INDIA COMPANY (The Honourable East India Company) in 1700. The arms of the company are drawn here in rose, black, and blue enamel colors with *rouge de fer.* They were copied from the company's bookplate. The decoration has often been copied on pieces of the so-called "Hong Kong" reproduction porcelain. Not to be confused with this inferior ware, however, is a second early service made in underglaze blue. OL: 10¾″ (27.3 cm); OW: 7⅞″ (20 cm).

Oval platter, Chia Ch'ing, c. 1810, British market. This is a piece from the only known service made for the British market in orange "Fitzhugh" style. The crest of NESBITT and motto, "Je le Maintiendrai," were painted in England. The service was probably ordered by Thomas Nesbitt of Lismore, County Cavan, Ireland. OL: 19″ (48.3 cm); OW: 16⅜″ (41.7 cm).

25

26

Plate, Kuang Hsü, c. 1897, Portuguese market. This is
more properly a commemorative rather than an
armorial piece. It celebrates the fourth centenary of
the Portuguese discovery of India by Vasco da Gama
during his 1497–99 voyage. The Portuguese ships or
carracks are painted in polychrome enamel colors
and are encircled with the inscription "Quarto Cen-
tenario Do Descobrimento de India." Diam: 9¾"
(24.8 cm).

II. Floral Decoration

The special attraction of floral-decorated porcelain is hard to deny. Designs of flowers and other such naturalistic elements as trees and fruits have long been a staple of china painters around the world. No one country has a clear claim to originality of expression. Objects decorated in this manner during the Yung Chêng and early Ch'ien Lung periods in China in *famille rose* enamels are especially outstanding. They have a luminous beauty in their coloring and shading and a finely-executed, free-hand line. It is perhaps only natural that the Chinese should have excelled at this type of decoration for it forms an important part of their aesthetic tradition. In treating floral-decorated porcelain for the export market, we are also dealing with ware intended for the domestic market if not the Imperial Court itself. The Chinese language of flowers was also influenced by other Oriental cultures, particularly the Japanese with their Kakiemon and Imari-decorated wares, but it retained an almost unique symbolic vocabulary.

Porcelain decorated in this manner is rarely treated by scholars. There are those who dismiss it in the following way: "Most of it appears to be a perfectly frank and unmistakable imitation of English models which were, no doubt, sent to China to be copied by Oriental artists."[1] This may be true of late eighteenth and early nineteenth-century ware; it is not the case with finer Yung Chêng pieces. The whole matter of design attribution raises the classic problem of the "chicken and the egg"—which came first? Producers of Dutch and English Delft or tin-glazed earthenware discovered Chinese design sources of the floral variety in the seventeenth century. In the resulting interchange of forms and patterns between East and West, national lines were considerably obscured. There is no question but that Delft examples were brought to China and that these were, to some extent, "copied" by potters and decorators, but the latter were clearly working within a tradition with which they were familiar and accomplished. Only later in the century do we witness an almost slavish devotion to European floral motifs as found on Meissen, Sèvres, and English objects.

In terms of the body of the work itself only one process required special mention. This method is illustrated by the extremely delicate eggshell porcelains, figures 27 and 28, which, in technique, dates from the Ming dynasty. The Chinese term this effect produced by working the clay, *t'o-t'ai*, and this translates as "without a body." As D. F. Lunsingh Scheurleer notes, "Sometimes the body is so thin that the outside and inside glazes seem to touch."[2] European porcelain of the same sort is imitative of the Chinese and is worked in a similar manner.

The Imari-style decoration, as seen in figure 31 (included here because it combines floral and landscape motifs), is often confused with the Japanese. As mentioned here and elsewhere, the Chinese produced a ware that was considerably thinner in body and clearer in color. Thus, while imitative, it represents a distinct Chinese type.

The number of known floral patterns is considerable. Those which are most commonly encountered are the "Lotus," "Tobacco Leaf," and "Cabbage Leaf." Such motifs as the chrysanthemum, peony, strawberry, cherry, gardenia, and poppy are used in various combinations as well as singly. Trees such as the willow were to become a staple of export ware; the plum tree in bloom and the bamboo are also found. Water lilies, iris, and such fruits as the peach, pomegranate, and quince are frequently used. Of all the aforementioned, the "Lotus," as seen in figure 30 and in the service illustrated in color in plates VII and XIII, emerges as a favorite of today's collectors. Enormous amounts of ware bearing this flower, a symbol of summer and of the month of July in Chinese iconography, must have been shipped to the West. The very special pink shade achieved by the decorators has long attracted Westerners. Other seasonal flowers are the peony (spring), chrysanthemum (fall), and plum blossom or prunus (winter).

The peony occurs in combination with the lotus in figure 30, with strawberries in figure 34, and on the garniture set, color plate XII. It is an emblem of good fortune and feminine beauty, and if presented in triple form, stands for extra good luck. The modern variety of the peony is, of course, a garden plant which reached Europe from China. The chrysanthemum, figure 27, is a motif more often found on Japanese porcelains, but it, too, formed a part of the traditional Chinese floral vocabulary. Many of the flowers are used with bird, animal or insect figures, among them being the peacock, figure 29, butterflies, figures 35 and 39, and unidentified bugs, figure 39.

The "Tobacco Leaf" pattern is employed in several different palettes, but is seen in plate VIII in green and blue and orange. The pattern seems to have been introduced during the mid-1700s and continued in vogue well into the 1800s. It should not be confused with the "Cabbage Leaf" pattern illustrated in section XII, figure 143. Porcelain with the design of this sort was made primarily for the American market during the nineteenth century.

Late eighteenth-century pieces do exhibit greater reliance on European decorative motifs. The floral sprig seen on plates illustrated in figures 38 and 39 is a direct copy from European sources. These are more formal and less graceful renderings of a neo-classical sort. Some of these small bouquets or flowers arranged in an urn or basket must have found great favor among the style-conscious. Even more elaborate arrangements are described by Clare Le Corbeiller, and these were copied by the Chinese in gold and black in the fashion of engravings from the seventeenth-century *Livres de Plusieurs Paniers de Fleurs*.[3]

NOTES

[1] Homer Eaton Keyes, "Biblical and Floral Designs," *Chinese Export Porcelain*, ed. Elinor Gordon (New York: Universe Books, 1975), p. 31.

[2] D. F. Lunsingh Scheurleer, *Chinese Export Porcelain* (London: Faber and Faber, Ltd., 1974, and New York: Pitman Publishing Corp., 1974), p. 30.

[3] Clare Le Corbeiller, *China Trade Porcelain: Patterns of Exchange* (New York: Metropolitan Museum of Art, 1974), pp. 71–75.

27

Tea bowl and saucer, Yung Chêng, c. 1730, European market. A central chrysanthemum motif is surrounded by a wide border of lotus petals on the saucer. All the decoration is painted in *famille rose* colors on an eggshell porcelain. The tea bowl repeats the wide border design. OH (tea bowl): 1⅜″ (3.5 cm), Diam (top): 2⅝″ (6.7 cm); Diam (saucer): 4⅛″ (10.5 cm).

28

Tea bowl and saucer, Yung Chêng, c. 1730, European market. Different in design but similar in its successful use of *famille rose* colors is this set also executed in eggshell porcelain. The central design on the saucer is of a vase and flowers and is surrounded by a scalloped Y-diaper border. The second and wide cell diaper border contains three framed reserves with flowers, and this is surrounded by an outer diaper border. The tea bowl repeats the border designs with three framed floral reserves. OH (tea bowl): 1⅜″ (3.5 cm), Diam (top): 2⅝″ (6.7 cm); Diam (saucer): 4¼″ (16.6 cm).

29

Tea bowl and saucer, Ch'ien Lung, c. 1740, European market. The peacock is an often encountered decorative element on mid-eighteenth-century export ware. It is drawn here with a black body, blue-green enamel wings, gilt tail feathers, and green and red eyes. The "Laub-und-Bandelwerk" border, a design motif derived from Meissen porcelains, is worked in gilt. Such a border often incorporates the figure of a peacock, but in this example the decorator has used the bird for the primary decoration. OH (tea bowl): 1½" (3.8 cm), Diam (top): 2¹⁵⁄₁₆" (7.5 cm); Diam (saucer): 4⁹⁄₁₆" (11.7 cm).

Octagonal plate, Ch'ien Lung, c. 1750, European market. Peonies and a lotus share the center of this plate with a landscape scroll. The same handsome flower and scroll motif is repeated in the border. The details of the landscape scenes in the center and the border are clearly Chinese rather than European. All the decoration is executed in polychrome enamel colors with underglaze blue and gilt. Diam: 8⅞″ (22.6 cm).

30

Plate, Ch'ien Lung, c. 1750, European market. This example is decorated in the "Imari style." Japanese export porcelains made at Arita and shipped from the port of Imari were characteristically decorated in underglaze blue, *rouge de fer,* and gilt, as is this piece. The style was popular in the late seventeenth century and was used by the Chinese for some of their own export wares beginning in the eighteenth century. Chinese wares are distinguished by being thinner and clearer of color than those of the Japanese. The scene of houses and shrubbery near a river running before a crenelated wall is unusual in Chinese Imari ware. Diam: 8¹³⁄₁₆″ (22.5 cm).

31

Plate, Ch'ien Lung, c. 1755, European market. A vibrant turquoise color provides the ground for a central design of white latch hooks and dots outlined in black. The inner cell diaper border contains four floral reserves. Decorating the rim are clusters of flowers and some of the "Eight Precious Objects" of Chinese mythology. Diam: 8⅞" (20 cm).

33

Cream jug with attached lid, Ch'ien Lung, c. 1750, European market. To attach a lid by means of a chain was not at all uncommon; hinged lids are the exception. The jug is covered with flowers drawn in polychrome enamels, and these are surrounded by a cell diaper border. OH: 4⅝" (11.8 cm); OW (including handle): 3½" (8.9 cm).

32

Plate VI. Punch bowl, Ch'ien Lung, c. 1785, European market. The harvesting and stacking of wheat in the European manner has been captured by a Chinese artist in brilliant polychrome enamel colors. Vignettes of landscapes rendered in *rouge de fer* on a gilt Y-diaper ground alternate with the scenes. The interior border is decorated in gilt, *rouge de fer* green, and black. In the bottom is found a floral spray worked in polychrome enamels. This bowl, made for the European market, is similar to one in the collection of the Metropolitan Museum. *See* Phillips, pl. 13. OH: 4½″ (11.5 cm), Top Diam (top): 11¼″ (28.5 cm).

Plate VII. Foreground, cream jug with lid, teabowl, cup and saucer, teapot; *Background,* dish, bowl, cup and saucer, dish, Ch'ien Lung, c. 1760, European market. The popular eighteenth-century Lotus design appeared in several different variations. All the pieces here, except for the dishes in the background, display a gilt floral sprig in a gilt spear bordered reserve against a ground of brilliant rose-colored lotus petals. The lotus petal was used in a similar manner to decorate ware from the "Six Dynasties" period (220–587 A.D.). *See* Phillips, pl. 78. Cream jug with lid—OH: 5″ (12.7 cm); teabowl—OH: 2⅞″ (7.3 cm), Diam (top): 3⁵⁄₁₆″ (8.4 cm); cup and saucer—OH (cup): 2⁹⁄₁₆″ (6.6 cm), Diam (saucer): 4⅝″ (11.8 cm); teapot—OH: 5¼″ (13.3 cm), OL: (including handle) 7½″ (19.1 cm); dishes—Diam: 8¹⁄₁₆″ (20.6 cm); bowl—OH: 2⅝″ (6.7 cm), Diam (top): 5¹¹⁄₁₆″ (14.5 cm); cup and saucer—OH (cup): 2½″ (6.4 cm), Diam (saucer): 4⁹⁄₁₆″ (11.7 cm).

Plate VIII. Covered tureen and stand, Ch'ien Lung, c. 1760, European market. Tobacco Leaf designs were most popular during the mid-eighteenth century but continued in production until at least 1800. Large green and underglaze blue serrated leaves with polychrome enamel flowers cover the surface of both the covered tureen and stand. A thin underglaze blue band follows the scalloped rim of the cover and of the stand. On the reverse side of the stand around the rim are found four floral groups in orange and underglaze blue. OH (covered tureen): 5⅛″ (13 cm), OL: 11⅛″ (28.2 cm). OW: 8″ (20.4 cm). OH (stand): 9³⁄₁₈″ (23.4 cm), OW: 12⅛″ (30.8 cm).

Plate IX. "Fitzhugh" plates and dishes, Chia Ch'ing, c. 1800–1815, American or English market. The designation "Fitzhugh" refers to a pattern consisting of a central medallion, four surrounding panels of floral design representing the Chinese arts, and a repeating border design of diapering, butterflies, flowers, trellis, and a Greek-key fret. Underglaze blue is the most common color motif, and yellow one of the most rare. *Left foreground,* underglaze blue, Diam: 9⅞" (25.1 cm); brown, Diam: 9⅝" (24.5 cm); green and orange, Diam: 9¹¹⁄₁₆ (24.7 cm); yellow, Diam: 8½" (21.7 cm). *Right background,* black, Diam: 9⅞" (25.1 cm); green, Diam: 9" (22.9 cm); blue and gilt, Diam: 9½" (24.2 cm); brown and green, Diam: 9¾" (24.8 cm).

Plate X. Left, "Baptism of Christ" plate, Yung Chêng, c. 1725, Dutch market, Diam: 10¾" (27.3 cm); "Crucifixion" plate, Ch'ien Lung, c. 1740, European market, Diam: 8⅞" (22.6 cm). *Right,* "Nativity" plate, Ch'ien Lung, c. 1740, European market, Diam: 9" (22.9 cm); "Resurrection" plate, Ch'ien Lung, c. 1740, European market, Diam: 9¹⁄₁₆" (23.1 cm).

Mugs, decorated and undecorated, Ch'ien Lung, c. 1760, European market. An example of an undecorated piece of export ware is seen at right. The raised panels would have been painted with floral sprays as on the piece at left. The panels and flowered vines are glazed. The background has been decorated, however, with tiny touches of a thick white glaze. "Chicken skin" is a term often used to describe this type of porcelain. The handle has been shaped in the form of a dragon. OH: 4⅞" (12.4 cm), OW (including handle): 5½" (14 cm).

Decorators in Canton applied butterflies and flowers in rose, lavender, green, and orange enamel to the glazed panels at left. These are raised on a "chicken skin" ground. The border is gilt, and there is a Greek key band on an orange enamel ground. OH: 4¹³⁄₁₆" (12.2 cm), OL: 6¼" (15.8 cm).

Mug, Ch'ien Lung, c. 1760, European market. Imaginatively delineated and lushly colored strawberries and peonies in polychrome enamels, *rouge de fer*, and gilt surround this handsome object. A design of a branching trunk has been worked in underglaze blue. OH: 5½" (14 cm).

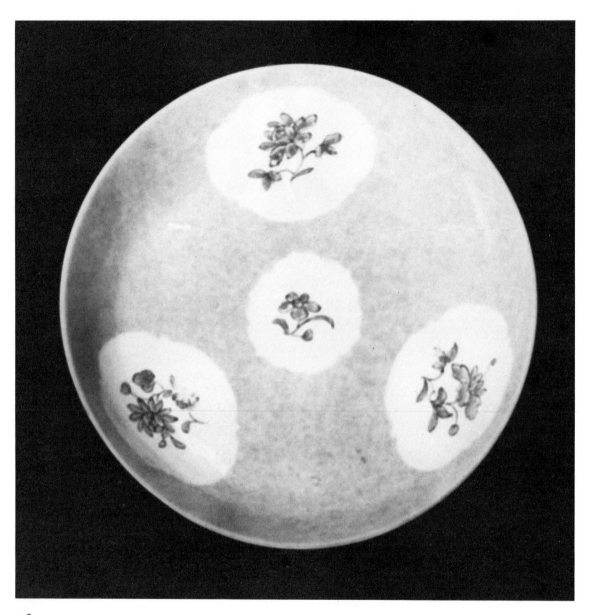

36   Saucer, Ch'ien Lung, c. 1760, European market. A soft, mottled, turquoise base is the ground for four gilt floral sprigs in reserves. The decoration is in the style of Sèvres wares; a turquoise blue color (*bleu celeste*) was first developed at Sèvres in 1752. Diam: 4⅝" (11.8 cm).

Plate, Ch'ien Lung, c. 1770, European market. Small sprays of flowers in polychrome enamels decorate the center of this plate with an openwork edge and basketweave texture which extends across the surface. Many of the European faience and porcelain manufacturers made tablewares with an open (and closed) basketweave border. A piece of Meissen may have been copied in this particular case. Diam: 9¾₁₆″ (23.4 cm).

37

Plate, Ch'ien Lung, c. 1770, European market. Extremely unusual in export ware are any marks of a maker. Seen here to the right of the center is a small Chinese character incised into the clay on the face of the plate. This mark could also stand for the name of the decorator. In other respects the object is typical of late eighteenth-century floral pattern porcelains with a small central sprig of flowers in polychrome enamels. The chain inner border is decorated in gilt; that of the double band outer border, magenta and blue with *rouge de fer* and gilt. Diam: 9⅝″ (24.5 cm).

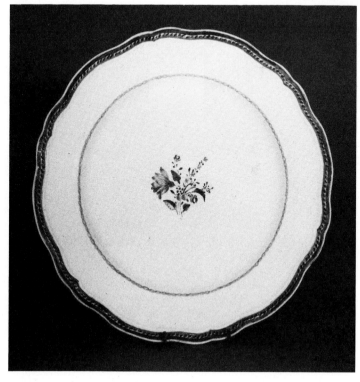

38

Plate, Ch'ien Lung, c. 1780, European market. Coming closer to European porcelains in decoration is this delicately painted plate. The floral spray and butterflies and insects are executed in polychrome enamel colors. The inner line border is executed in black; that of the outer sawtooth band is green. Diam: 9¼″ (23.5 cm).

Tea bowl and saucer, Ch'ien Lung, c. 1785, possibly Middle Eastern market. An extremely deep underglaze blue covers both the tea bowl and saucer. This is known as "Mazarine" blue. Over this is drawn a continuous pattern of flowers and leaves in a lightly applied gilt. Few pieces exist today with the gold still intact. The combination of colors and form is an imaginative concept somewhat foreign to the European market. OH (tea bowl): 2¾″ (7 cm), Diam (top): 3⅝″ (9.2 cm); Diam (saucer): 5⅛″ (13 cm).

39

40

41

Plate, Ch'ien Lung, c. 1790, Middle Eastern market. An Arabic inscription is borne in the center in lime-green enamel. It reads: "Mr. Abrahim Nejreehan," probably the man for whom the service was made. This is an old style of Arabic lettering in which the order of ciphers was rearranged for an artistic effect. Other known services made for the Middle Eastern market are decorated with verses of the Koran and other inscriptions. This piece also contains elaborate inner and outer flower band borders in polychrome enamel colors, *rouge de fer*, and gilt. Between them is a conventional floral band in blue enamel and *rouge de fer*. *See* Beurdeley, cat. 27 and pg. 17. Diam: 9¾" (24.8 cm).

III. Blue and White Decoration

Blue and white porcelain made during the K'ang Hsi (1662–1722) and Yung Chêng (1723–1735) periods is among the finest ware made for export to the West. Extremely rare today and almost priceless, it compares with later Canton and Nanking as night does with day. Production of underglaze blue ware began seriously during the Ming dynasty and probably reached its peak in the late seventeenth century after T'sang Ying-hsuan was appointed director of the Imperial factory in Ching-tê Chên. Unlike most of the eighteenth- and nineteenth-century porcelains decorated with polychrome enamels, those of early underglaze blue were produced entirely in Ching-tê Chên. In the words of D. F. Lunsingh Scheurleer, this was the "finest blue that was ever manufactured . . . even the simplest blue and white has its particular cachet."[1]

The ware being discussed and illustrated here was made primarily for the Dutch market. The Vereenigde Oostindische Compagnie (commonly referred to as the VOC) of Holland had entered the China trade as early as 1602, and it is estimated that at least three million pieces of porcelain had been brought to Europe from 1604 to 1657. Then, for nearly twenty years, trade with the VOC and other European merchants was cut off because of domestic turmoil. With the reestablishment of the kilns at Ching-tê Chên in 1683, production of the finest sort was given a fresh start. It was not to lose its essential fine character until at least the 1730s, although there are blue and white porcelains which are clearly inferior to those executed in more colorful palettes.

The early blue and white ware was not sent on to Canton for decoration for the simple reason that the decoration was applied before a glaze was added and the piece fired. The blue pigment, known as "Mohammedan blue" on Ming dynasty pieces, was derived from a cobaltiferous ore of manganese brought from the Near East. The pigment was mixed with water and painted on the clay with a brush. The most expertly decorated and fired pieces are those with a deep, rich, luminous blue covered by a very fine glaze. This is most evident in the deer figure illustrated in these pages, plate XIII. Those of an inferior quality display a dull blue marked by a glimmer of red or purplish tint.

The actual process of decoration was observed in the early eighteenth century by Father d'Entrecolles, a Jesuit missionary. He wrote in 1712 that "the Painting part is divided, in the same Work-house, among a great number of Operators. It is the sole Business of one to strike the first colour'd Circle, near the Edges of the Ware; another traces the Flowers, which are painted by a third; it belongs to one to draw Rivers and Mountains, to another Birds and other Animals: As for the Figures of Men, they are commonly the worst done of all."[2] He added later that the Chinese decorators often were required to copy European figures, a task for which they were clearly not suited. It is, indeed, surprising how well some of them succeeded with not only form but resemblance as they frequently had to work from imprecise samples brought to China by the Western traders.

Western figures were not always, of course, included in the decoration. They are present in the plate, figure 42, depicting the "Riots of Rotterdam" but completely absent from the later landscape scene, figure 44, showing houses in the Dutch style along a river. In large part, the motifs employed in blue and white K'ang Hsi and Yung Chêng wares remained basically Chinese. Armorial wares, of course, incorporated proper European heraldic symbols. The earliest of these wares in blue and white do not always successfully blend Oriental and Western armorial motifs. The Chinese decorative elements remain fairly simple—trees, branches, birds, animals, a flowing stream. The forms on which they are used are more clearly European—plates, bowls, vases with handles, pitchers, teapots, goblets. Some of the plates, if not other forms, are probably the last surviving pieces from full blue and white services.

Western influence in decoration is seen in the religious theme expressed in the "Charity" saucer, figure 43, one of a pair. A more widely used religious subject was that of the "Crucifixion," plate X, a scene later much copied in polychrome enamels as well as in *grisaille* or *encre de chine*. The decoration of the saucer is not to be confused, however, with that style now termed "Jesuit" which employed the *famille rose* palette and *encre de chine* or grisaille pencilling.

The "Riots in Rotterdam" plate is the earliest piece displayed here and is one of the most original of export patterns based on a European design. According to Clare Le Corbeiller, fourteen plates and two sets of cups and saucers are known to exist with this decoration. From this figure it is surmised that a fairly large number of pieces must have been produced.[3] The plate shown carries the reign mark of Ch'êng Hua (1465–1487), as do at least six other "Rotterdam" pieces. After 1677, use of the K'ang Hsi mark was forbidden, and porcelain makers reached back in time for something pseudo-historical. Eventually even such appropriated reign marks were to disappear, leaving the vast bulk of export ware completely without imprint.

The "Rotterdam" plate also contains some traditional Chinese decorative elements. Two of the reserves in the border contain *pa pao* symbols or the "Eight Precious Objects." These are difficult to identify precisely; their meaning is similarly subject to different interpretations. The eight have been variously catalogued as the pearl (chu), copper coin (ch'ien), lozenge (hua), open lozenge (feng shêng), musical stone (ch'ing), pair of books (shu), horn-like objects (chüeh), and leaf of artemisia (ai yeh).

The vast majority of collectors today can not expect to possess porcelains of such an early date and value. The study of them, however, in museums and other private collections contributes to one's understanding and appreciation of the finest in porcelain making. That these wares were copied by Dutch and English Delft manufacturers of the late seventeenth and eighteenth centuries is an unchallenged fact. These fine pieces provide the collector with a peerless yardstick against which to measure the later blue and white production—in Europe and China.

NOTES

[1] D. F. Lunsingh Scheurleer, *Chinese Export Porcelain* (London: Faber and Faber, Ltd., 1974, and New York: Pitman Publishing Corp., 1974), p. 74.

[2] Quoted in John Goldsmith Phillips, *China Trade Porcelain* (Cambridge, Mass.: Harvard University Press, 1956), p. 9.

[3] Clare Le Corbeiller, *China Trade Porcelain: Patterns of Exchange* (New York: The Metropolitan Museum of Art, 1974), p. 32.

42

Plate, K'ang Hsi, c. 1690, Dutch market. One of the oldest and best-known subjects of export ware decoration is the "Riots of Rotterdam," also called the "Costerman Revolt." A Dutchman named Costerman killed a servant of the tax collector on the night of August 28, 1690, in a fight resulting from his refusal to pay an excise duty on a cask of wine. He was sentenced to death on September 16, 1690. This so angered the people of Rotterdam that they took revenge on the first sheriff, Jacob van Zuylen van Nyevelt, by demolishing his house. Medals were struck in pewter, silver, and gold to commemorate the event, and some of these found their way to China to serve as a model for the subject on this plate. There are several versions, some showing three houses next to the sheriff's house, and others four.

All the decoration is, of course, executed in underglaze blue. The cell diaper border holds four reserves; two with flowers alternate with two enclosing *pa pao* symbols ("Eight Precious Objects"). The reverse of the rim is decorated by a lotus scroll with a swastika band. Found on the base is a mark of the Ch'êng Hua reign (1465-87) in a double ring. *See* Le Corbeiller, pg. 51, and Scheurleer, figs. 131, 132. Diam: 7¾" (19.7 cm).

Saucer, K'ang Hsi, c. 1710, Dutch market. "Charity," symbolized by the nursing mother, is the subject of this handsome object. The whole scene is rendered in underglaze blue. A small blue flower mark is found on the underside. *See* Le Corbeiller, pg. 28. Diam: 5⅜" (13.7 cm).

43

Octagonal plate, Ch'ien Lung, c. 1740, Dutch market. A Dutch landscape is drawn on this object in underglaze blue. The two hounds in the foreground look very much like those modeled in *blanc de chine* at roughly the same time. A platter in the same design was recently sold at Sotheby Parke-Bernet, New York, to the American Museum of the China Trade. Diam: 8⅜" (21.4 cm).

44

IV. Mythological and Religious Decoration

Religious and mythological or allegorical scenes from European sources are datable to at least the K'ang Hsi period. Popular demand for such porcelain did not, however, increase until the reign of Yung Chêng (1723–1735). In terms of quality production, the important years were 1730 to 1760 and include the early period of Emperor Ch'ien Lung (1735–1795). The development of biblical and mythological decoration parallels in many respects the introduction of opaque *famille rose* enamel colors and *encre de chine* or *grisaille* painting. The years in which T'ang Ying served as director of the Ching-tê Chên porcelain factories, 1736 to 1749 or 1753, were certainly critical for the mastery of European-style decoration.

Increasingly during the first half of the eighteenth century, Chinese symbols were replaced with European. It was only natural that this should happen as export ware was, as the Dutch and French style it, *chine de commande*, china made to order. The Chinese were more than willing to oblige foreign customers, and with the rise of porcelain production in Europe during the eighteenth century, they were, in effect, forced to compete with similar, popular designs. In many ways, the Chinese decorators responded with unusual enterprise to this challenge. Michel Beurdeley does not see this as being at all exceptional: "Old Chinese legends are full of symbols, and are peopled with imaginary figures to meet the needs of a naturally mystical people. . . . It is not surprising, therefore, to find that the Chinese had less difficulty in the interpretation of legendary scenes from Europe. In this world of fantasy, gods and goddesses could be subjected to the painter's imagination on subjects which were slightly more comprehensible to them than others from the West."[1]

How did the Chinese come by their inspiration? Authorities in the past have ascribed unusual influence to Jesuit missionaries who arrived in Ching-tê Chên in the early 1700s. It is clear that they carried with them engravings of biblical scenes, if only in the Bible itself, which could be copied. The Jesuits may have supplied other pieces of art as well, but to ascribe such power to this religious order, albeit famed for its Byzantine powers, is to tell only part of the story. To term export ware with religious decoration "Jesuit-style" porcelain, as has been done for years, is simply misleading.

The first religious subjects were decorated in underglaze blue and white during the K'ang Hsi period. According to Clare Le Corbeiller, "it is clear from peculiarities of style that the painted China trade porcelains were copies from painted examples of Protestant Dutch or English pottery."[2] Stylistic influences from the Dutch Delft factories are undeniable in the early period. Le Corbeiller calls the style of the Dutch "impromptu" and in the hands of the Oriental decorator, it was literally copied in what many find to be a naïve manner. Not until later, after the Chinese were already familiar with traditional Old and New Testament themes, did a more sophisticated style emerge. This more finished approach may, indeed, be ascribed with greater reason to the prompting of the Jesuit missionaries.

The writings of the most famous of these, Père d'Entrecolles, from Ching-tê Chên provide a primary source of information for today's scholars. His commentary on the first use of *encre de chine* decoration is particularly illuminating as it applies to export ware with religious scenes. In 1722 d'Entrecolles reported: "They have tried to paint porcelain vases with the finest Chinese black ink, but so far without success. When the porcelain had been fired the ink was too faint. The composition of this black is not strong enough to withstand the action of the fire, or perhaps it was not able to penetrate the glaze, or to produce a colour contrasting strongly enough with the glaze."[3] How exactly the Jesuits might have assisted the Chinese in perfecting the black linear method is a matter of pure conjecture. It does seem possible, however, that they supplied samples of continental European ware which employed a similar technique of black enamel decoration (*schwarzlot*) first used on faience by the Dutch in the mid-seventeenth century and later perfected by du Paquier in Vienna.

That the Chinese mastered the craft of using black decoration to heighten and define figures and forms in the manner of an engraving is amply demonstrated in plate X, the "Crucifixion" scene. Accompanying it in the same color illustration is an earlier plate, the "Baptism of Christ," which is decorated completely in *rouge de fer* with gilt. This latter piece reflects the earlier dependence on the Dutch Delft tradition while the former demonstrates a growing expertness with line and the use of a more sophisticated border decoration which borrows from the Viennese *laub-und-bandelwerk* in its strapwork.

Also seen in the same illustration are two of the other popular New Testament themes: "Nativity" and "Resurrection." Religious scenes executed in polychrome enamels are very rare, and represent the last in a series of decorative steps beginning with underglaze blue and white. Exactly why biblical scenes were most often painted in a less brilliant manner is a matter of speculation. Perhaps their very sober nature called for a more conservative approach. In addition to the New Testament stories, there were those from the Old Testament. "Rebecca at the Well," figure 51, was one of the most popular and appeared on cups and saucers as well as plates. "Adam and Eve" is known to have been used for decoration in underglaze blue during the K'ang Hsi period, and is shown here in *encre de chine* with sepia details, figure 50. Among other Old Testament stories found on export ware are "Susanna and the Elders," "Noah and His Daughters," and "Joseph and Potiphar's Wife." Nearly all the early to mid-eighteenth century export ware with religious decoration appears to have been directed to Holland and other continental European markets.

The history of export ware with mythological decoration is similar to that of the religious but seems somewhat more dependent on the development of the *famille rose* palette of enamel colors. Mythological or allegorical scenes are found on pieces with underglaze blue decoration, figure 45, but those decorated in polychrome enamels, if not common, are at least not as rare as the religious subjects. Stories from classical mythology became great favorites in eighteenth-century Europe, and the Chinese decorators could turn to such artists as Lancret, Watteau, and Albani, and the engravings based on their paintings for very direct inspiration.

The imaginative use of the soft *famille rose* colors is seen in "Water," figure 46, one of four plates representing the elements and based on an engraving of a painting by Francesco Albani. Seen with this subject is a second, "Earth." According to Beurdeley, these porcelains were executed for different customers at varying times, but all are painted with *famille rose* decoration. Director T'ang Ying termed this form of decoration "painting of white porcelain with enamel in the way of the Westerners."[4] This is clearly what the Westerners wanted. The Chinese decorators of the Yung Chêng and the early Ch'ien Lung periods imbued the shades of pink and carmine derived from chloride of gold with a soft delicacy, a pale beauty that has rarely been matched since.

Renderings of mythological scenes in black or *encre de chine* and gilt continued in vogue until the 1780s. The "marriage party" plate, figure 52, is, according to Scheurleer, "probably the earliest datable example of decoration in *encre de chine* found in the Netherlands."[5] The Chinese artist's ability to delineate the fine lines of such a piece in the style of Meissen is clearly evidenced here. Other mythological or allegorical scenes of considerable popularity were the "Judgment of Paris," "Leda and the Swan," "Venus and Hermes," "Amor and Psyche," "Apollo and Diana," "Europa and the Bull," "The Toilet of Venus," "Perseus and Andromeda," and the "Altar of Love" or "Valentine," the last being one of the few datable patterns based on an English drawing, figure 54.

NOTES

[1] Michel Beurdeley, *Chinese Trade Porcelain* (Rutland, Vermont, and Tokyo, Japan: Charles E. Tuttle Co., 1962), p. 58.

[2] Clare Le Corbeiller, *China Trade Porcelain: Patterns of Exchange* (New York: The Metropolitan Museum of Art, 1974), p. 69.

[3] Quoted in Beurdeley, p. 59.

[4] Quoted in D. F. Lunsingh Scheurleer, *Chinese Export Porcelain* (London: Faber and Faber, Ltd., 1974, and New York: Pitman Publishing Corp., 1974), p. 79.

[5] *Ibid.*, p. 155.

Tea bowl and saucer, Yung Chêng, c. 1730, European market. Underglaze blue and white is an appropriate medium for this early rendering of the god Neptune holding his trident aloft, astride dolphins. The Dutch artist Abraham Bloemaert (1564-1651) collected several hundred of his drawings, genre scenes, figures, landscapes, and mythological and religious subjects to be used as a copybook for artists. In this case the Chinese porcelain decorator used the left half of one of Bloemaert's compositions and probably worked from an engraving of the subject by the Dutch artist's son, Frederick. *See* Le Corbeiller, pg. 66. OH (tea bowl): 2⅝″ (6.7 cm); Diam (saucer): 5⅝″ (14.3 cm).

Plates, Ch'ien Lung, c. 1740, European market. The elements—water, air, earth, and fire—are represented in a set of four plates, these being, water, at left, and earth. Both are drawn in polychrome enamels. The plate at left showing Venus riding in a rococo shell-shaped boat has a gilt scroll band border; that to the right with Ceres and three attendants riding in a chariot has a blue scroll band border. Francesco Albani (1578-1660?) painted these subjects several times, most notably for the Borghese Palace. The paintings were engraved by different artists through the years, and the decoration of these export plates is a simplification of the engraved designs. *See* Beurdeley, cat. 129. Diam: 8⅞″ (22.6 cm).

47

Plate, Ch'ien Lung, c. 1740, European market. Zeus and his wife, Hera, with their animal attributes, the eagle and the peacock, cavort on a rocky outcropping beside two putti. All is decorated in black, with a gilt inner border and a gilt and black outer border. Zeus is the supreme ruler of the Greek gods, the lord of the winds, the clouds, rain, and thunder. Hera, as goddess of marriage and maternity, presides over all phases of feminine existence. Diam: 9″ (22.9 cm).

48

Cup and saucer, Ch'ien Lung, c. 1740, European market. The goddess Juno is drawn in black with gilt and is seated on a cloud with a peacock at her side. The elaborate border found on the saucer and the cup is derived from a Viennese "Laub-und-bandelwerk" design of the early eighteenth century. It includes strapwork, scale diapering, festoons, and peacocks. Some saucers of this design have a fluted border rather than this more elaborate sort. Diam (saucer): 4¾" (12.1 cm).

Cup, Ch'ien Lung, c. 1745, European market. Polychrome enamels are used exclusively in this object which features a scene of Caesar reaching out his hand to Cleopatra before a triumphal arch. Camels and their riders are found in the left background. OH: 2¹¹⁄₁₆″ (4.3 cm).

Tea bowl and saucer, Ch'ien Lung, c. 1740, European market. The biblical scene of Eve handing the apple to Adam with the serpent in the tree is drawn in black with sepia details. The leaf scroll border is of gilt. This subject was treated earlier during the K'ang Hsi period in blue and white and later in polychrome enamels. *See* Scheurleer, pl. 234 and Beurdeley, cat. 57. OH (tea bowl): 1½″ (3.8 cm); Diam (saucer): 4½″ (11.4 cm).

49

50

51

Plate, Ch'ien Lung, c. 1740, European market. The Genesis story of Rebecca at the well is the subject of this handsomely-decorated plate. The central scene is painted in polychrome enamels and is surrounded by a plain gilt band. Four groups of flowers and leafy vines decorate the rim. Seen at Rebecca's right is Eliezer, who had been sent by his master, Abraham, to select a suitable bride for his son Isaac. The subject is one of the most popular in early export ware, and all examples in porcelain seem to be derived from the same European print source. Ex coll. William Martin-Hurst. Diam: 8¹⁵⁄₁₆″ (22.8 cm).

52

Plate, Ch'ien Lung, c. 1745, European market. A wedding scene such
as this appears only on plates. Most probably the objects were intended
as presentation pieces and were not made in sets. The title page of an
eighteenth-century wedding song is the known source for the scene. Here
a wedding party is gathered together within an architectural setting
while tritons and nymphs frolic in the foreground. On the arch is the
blessing "Semper amor pro te firmissimus atrue fidelis." The arms of
two Dortrecht families, perhaps those of the wedding couple, BEAUMONT
and BACKUS, are displayed above the cornices at either side. All the
decoration is executed in black with flesh tones. The gilt lacework
border is in the style of Meissen ware. *See* Cox, pg. 599 and pl. 169.
Diam: 8⅞" (22.6 cm).

53

Plate, Ch'ien Lung, c. 1745-60, European market. This plate
illustrates one scene from a series depicting couples from
classical mythology. The central scene is drawn in polychrome enamel colors and sepia. The border of four large
floral sprays is executed in polychrome enamels. *See* Scheurleer, pl. 233. Diam: 9 1/16" (23.1 cm).

54

Bowl, Ch'ien Lung, c. 1760, possibly English market. The popular "Altar of Love" pattern, also referred to as the "Valentine" pattern, is here executed in polychrome enamels with gilt. Two scenes alternate with polychrome enamel floral sprays. The pattern for this decoration was probably a drawing by Peircy Brett made while he was in Canton in 1743. English china decorators at the Worcester factory later adapted it to their use. The interior of the bowl has three floral panels in underglaze blue around the sides and an enameled floral spray in the bottom. *See* Phillips, pl. 67 and fig. 48. OH: $3^{15}/_{16}$" (10 cm), Diam (top): $9^{3}/_{8}$" (23.9 cm).

V. European and Oriental Genre Scenes

Chinese export porcelain bearing various scenic motifs is among the most captivating and historically interesting of the wares produced in the seventeenth, eighteenth, and early nineteenth centuries. These are the genre scenes—European and Oriental—appearing on a wide variety of forms which have fascinated expert and amateur for many years. As Homer Eaton Keyes wrote, "Sometimes the workmanship is exquisite; sometimes it is relatively coarse and ungainly. But, whatever its failures in the essentials of draftsmanship, it is always interesting, always decorative."[1] The earliest of these objects were decorated in underglaze blue at Ching-tê Chên in the late 1600s, and are among the most valuable of all export artifacts. These have been discussed in part III, "Blue and White." Our particular interest here is the polychrome enamelled wares of the Yung Chêng, Ch'ien Lung, and Chia Ch'ing periods, most of which were decorated in Canton. Some were custom-made; the majority were produced in fairly large numbers for unknown customers throughout Europe, the Americas, and the Middle East.

The number of genre scenes must number at least in the several thousands. If one includes religious, mythological, and allegorical subjects, a subject treated in part IV, the number would have to be measurably increased. There seems to be little doubt that executed designs date from the mid-1700s, a period when decorators were perfecting their mastery of the *famille rose* palette and refining the technique of *encre de chine* painting. To the modern eye, many of these designs appear somewhat child-like if not naïve. "It is worth remembering," Michel Beurdeley comments, "that the rules of seventeenth-century Chinese painting rigorously denied the use of shadows and facial expressions to the artist, and his apparent naïveté is often nothing more than an attempt to abide by this strict Eastern aesthetic."[2] This does not mean that the Chinese decorator was necessarily less expert than the average European artist of the same sort. When presented with a subject closer to the traditional Chinese, such as the Pronk "Parasol" design, figure 72, the Canton painter was likely to excel. As noted in the caption to this illustration, Cornelius Pronk was commissioned to produce a design that could be used on export ware, and he turned to a theme inspired by a traditional K'ang Hsi subject. As Beurdeley notes, "The figures and birds lose all their Oriental character in the hands of the Dutchman. The Chinese artist on the other hand, while remaining faithful to the model, unknown to himself, rediscovers the elegance and precision of the East. The figures are less stiff, the decoration freer and more balanced."[3]

It must be kept in mind that the Chinese were not producing such porcelain for domestic use but for Western customers. During the eighteenth century Western themes were favored over the Oriental, a situation which would be reversed in the 1800s. The Chinese potters and decorators were engaged in stiff competition with those of Germany, Holland, England, and France, and models from various centers of ceramic production were carried to China for copying. At this time and until the late 1700s, fine Chinese wares were still cheaper in price than those produced in Europe. In addition to actual porcelain objects, the Chinese were also supplied with drawings and engravings to be followed. Among them are some of the most fanciful and inspired of subjects based on works by Watteau, Lancret, Picart, Baudoin, and a group of English artists. The Chinese were, indeed, good copy artists, but they were even better as synthesizers of various elements, and the end result of such resourceful use of elements was, in itself, a distinctly different object. Clare Le Corbeiller, in describing the cup and saucer illustrated in figure 65, says this particularly well: "Most China trade porcelain represents a compilation of elements—a pictorial fragment from one source, a border pattern from another, the model itself from a third. . . ."[4]

Such a scene as the "Cherrypickers" is found on numerous plates and tea services. The "Embroideress," also known as the "Seamstress," figure 61, recurs time and time again. The "Fishing Boy," figure 60, and the "Jugglers," figure 74, were obvious favorites with European customers. Designs such as these must have been carried in stock by the Canton merchants over a fairly long period of time. Such simple subjects were especially favored by the Dutch, and the amount of copying back and forth between Holland potters and those of China must have been as confusing then as it appears to be now, in retrospect.

Other genre scenes are less frequently encountered today and were probably more limited in production. They remain, however, basically commercial in nature and were not specially ordered and decorated items. The "Trumpeter's" cream jug, figure 55, is one of the earliest and is one of the few objects illustrated in *famille noire*. The design itself dates from the K'ang Hsi period. Nearly as rare is the Scottish Highlanders plate, figure 58, which features several victims of a Jacobite uprising in 1743. As Clare Le Corbeiller notes, a surprisingly large number of these plates survive today. The collector, however, can not expect to find many of them offered for sale. A cup and saucer in imitation of a Meissen style popular in the mid-eighteenth century, figure 65, was probably also produced in fairly large quantities, but only three other sets are known to exist in addition to that illustrated here, and these are in the Metropolitan Museum, the Mottahedeh collection, and the Victoria and Albert Museum. "Governor Duf" scenes were as popular as those of the "gallants" found on the cup and saucer, and the identity of the figures on such an object as the teapot, figure 73, will always cause argument among the experts. D. F. Lunsingh Scheurleer, a Dutch historian, seems to be closest to the truth: "The scene of a lady and a gentleman in eighteenth-century dress . . . dates from the end of the K'ang Hsi period . . . Some people choose to see Louis XIV and Madame de Maintenon in this walking couple, but in fact they must be Dutch rather than a French pair." Scheurleer, a good student of his country's past, then adds, "This is indicated by their dress, which is not smart and gay enough to warrant such an attribution. In the Netherlands this subject is sometimes called the 'Portrait of a happy Fries couple.' "[5] So much for the French court or the misnamed Governor.

One other group of porcelains of a fairly popular nature are the miniature tea sets as represented by the "After School" group, figure 78. These are an especially charming and successfully decorated ensemble. This is but one of two known sets based on paintings by Thomas Stothard, R. A., Keyes noted a third, "Playing at Marbles," which he claims was derived from Bartolozzi's mezzotint after William Hamilton's picture.[6]

We are left, then, with truly exceptional objects which must have been decorated on demand. Their numbers today are minuscule, and prices, if given at all, are similarly rarefied. Chief among these is the golfing plate, figure 59, a somewhat crude but singular item. Much more accomplished are two pieces from a service decorated with anatomical drawings, figures 66 and 67. These are based on drawings by J. A. Kulmus published in 1731. Further information regarding other pieces of this set is to be found in Arlene Palmer's recent guide for the Winterthur Museum.[7]

NOTES

[1] Homer Eaton Keyes, "Genre Designs," *Chinese Export Porcelain,* ed. Elinor Gordon (New York: Universe Books, 1975) , p. 36.

[2] Michel Beurdeley, *Chinese Trade Porcelain* (Rutland, Vermont: Charles E. Tuttle Co., 1962), p. 52.

[3] Clare Le Corbeiller, *China Trade Porcelain: Patterns of Exchange* (New York: Metropolitan Museum of Art, 1974), p. 93.

[4] Beurdeley, p. 57.

[5] D. F. Lunsingh Scheurleer, *Chinese Export Porcelain* (London: Faber and Faber, Ltd., 1974 and New York: Pitman Publishing Corp., 1974) , pp. 136-7.

[6] Keyes, p. 34.

[7] Arlene Palmer, *A Winterthur Guide to Chinese Export Porcelain* (New York: Crown Publishers, Inc., 1976), pp. 88-9.

55 Cream jug with lid, Yung Chêng, c. 1735, European market. Black enamel ground ware (*famille noire*) of the rare sort represented here was most popular during the preceding reign of K'ang Hsi. It was produced by covering a black glaze with green to deepen the effect. Because of the design, the pattern is known as the "Trumpeter's Service." The figure, apparently a Persian musician, is drawn in light blue, yellow, and brown against the black. The spear border is in gilt. A second known service contains pieces which are without the gold spear border. *See* Scheurleer, pl. 92. OH: 4⅞" (12.4 cm), OW: 4" (10.2 cm).

56

Cup and saucer, Ch'ien Lung, c. 1740,
European market. This harbor scene with
figures and ships and the surrounding
elaborate frame are drawn in polychrome
enamel colors with sepia and black. The
decoration was adapted from a Meissen
porcelain design popular c. 1730–35. Development of the design at Meissen
marked a change of interest away from
Chinese subjects in favor of European
scenes. OH (cup): 2⅝" (6.7 cm); Diam
(saucer): 5⅝" (14.3 cm).

Plate, Ch'ien Lung, c. 1750, European
market. The European village scene showing people gathered around a set of stocks
is rendered in polychrome enamel colors
and sepia with details in black. The spear
border is in gilt. Diam: 9" (22.9 cm).

57

58   Plate, Ch'ien Lung, c. 1745, Scottish market. The figures of two Scottish Highlanders drawn in polychrome enamels, *rouge de fer*, and black, one with bagpipes and the other with rifle, fill the center of this plate. Four gold scrolled cartouches around the rim enclose landscapes and birds in black. The two figures, a piper and a private in the Highland Regiment of the British Army (later known as the Black Watch) are copied from a set of four prints made by John Bowles c. 1743. In that year three privates and a piper, Macdonnel or Macdonald, deserted in the Stuart cause. The privates were executed and the piper sent to Georgia as a convict. The figures on this plate include Piper Macdonnel and probably one of the three privates. Diam: 87/8" (22.6 cm).

59   Plate, Chia Ch'ing, c. 1800, British market. The golfing scenes found on this object are extremely rare if not unique in export ware. Crudely drawn and positioned, they make up in charm what is missing in subtlety or sophistication. The players are painted wearing rose and blue shirts and white trousers. The gold course is sepia colored and the sky is painted in blue. Golfers today will note the unseemly bent elbows of the players. Diam: 9⅝" (24.5 cm).

60

Plate, Ch'ien Lung, c. 1740, European market. Blue,
green, yellow, and brown enamel colors are those
used in this scene of a boy fishing. Four landscape
medallions in *rouge de fer* alternate with gilt chry-
santhemums on the black and gilt cell diaper ground
of the border. The scene is copied from a drawing by
Abraham Bloemaert (1564–1651), first engraved by
his son Frederick (1610–c. 1669), and then by others.
The same design appears in objects decorated in rose
enamel, in *encre de chine*, and in underglaze blue.
Diam: 10 3/16″ (25.9 cm).

Bowl, Ch'ien Lung, c. 1760, European market, possibly Dutch. Two large oval panels, one on each side, frame a woman sewing beside a window which looks out on a harbor with ships. The design is one commonly encountered in export ware and has become known as "The Embroideress." The decoration is all in black with gilt details except for a light touching in red of the woman's lips. *See* Phillips, pls. 9 and 58. Diam: 5½" (14 cm), OH: 2½" (6.4 cm).

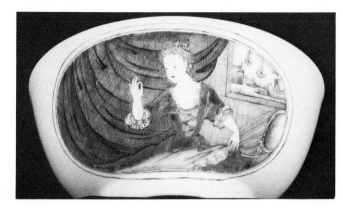

61

Punch bowl, Ch'ien Lung, c. 1760, English market. A continuous scene of a hunt is executed in polychrome enamels and sepia with green as the predominant color. Gilt spear borders decorate the base and the inside rim. Painted inside the bottom of the bowl is a horse and rider in polychrome enamels. This is one of many hunt scenes taken from prints by T. Burford after pictures by J. Seymour, c. 1750. OH: 6⅝" (16.8 cm), Diam (top): 16" (40.7 cm).

62

63

64

Covered butter dish and stand, Ch'ien Lung, c. 1775, European market. This scene of two women and a man gathering cherries into a large basket on the ground is painted in polychrome enamels with a twisted gilt chain border. The scene, known as the "Cherry Pickers," is found on many different export ware objects. It was taken from a print by Nicolas Ponce after a painting by Antoine Baudoin which, in turn, inspired François Boucher's large painting found at Kenwood in England. *See* Beurdeley, figs. 27–29, and Scheurleer, figs. 212–214. OH: 2½" (6.4 cm), OL: 5⁵⁄₁₆" (13.5 cm).

Tea bowl and saucer, Ch'ien Lung, c. 1790, American or English market. A farmyard scene in sepia and dark brown shows the feeding of a hen and baby chicks within a cage. The monogram *HT* is painted in gilt below the scene on the saucer and on the reverse of the tea bowl. The borders are in gilt. Diam (saucer): 3⁷⁄₁₆" (8.7 cm); OH (tea bowl): 2" (5.1 cm).

65

Cup and saucer, 1750–1800, European market. A form and design more mid-eighteenth-century European than Oriental is found in these two pieces. Four panels on each of the four-lobed objects are decorated alternately with scenes of young galants paying court to their young ladies and floral sprays on yellow ground. The amorous scenes are painted in polychrome colors on white ground. All the panels are bordered with white gilt scrolls. A small floral spray is found in the center of the saucer. The inner border of the cup is worked in Meissen style with a gilt lacework band. The monogram mark *AR,* for Elector Augustus Rex, in imitation of Meissen ware, is painted on the base of each piece. Only two other examples of such cups and saucers are known, one pair being in the collection of the Metropolitan Museum of Art. *See* Le Corbeiller, pgs. 92 and 93. OH (cup) : 3¼" (8.2 cm) ; saucer: 5½" (14 cm) x 4¹⁵⁄₁₆" (12.5 cm) .

Covered cream jug, Ch'ien Lung, 1761, Dutch market. This piece and a second that follows are part of what was probably a unique tea service decorated with anatomical drawings taken from *Tabulae Anatomicae* by J. A. Kulmus (Amsterdam, 1731). All of the drawings are in *encre de chine*. The first design is of a full skeleton and various skeletal parts. Leaves and berries border the top rim of the jug, lid, and handle. The Henry Francis du Pont Winterthur Museum export ware collection contains three other pieces from this service—a sugar bowl lid, cup, and saucer. The lid bears what may be the name of the owner, *Eleun Lira*, and a date, *1761*, which may be that of the year of decoration. A second saucer is in a private collection. *See* Palmer, pg. 88. OH (with cover): 5" (12.7 cm).

66

Cup, Ch'ien Lung, 1761, Dutch market. The drawings, in *encre de chine*, are three views of a fetus. The same berry and leaf border found on the cream jug is duplicated here. OH: 2⁷⁄₁₆" (6.2 cm).

67

68

Plate, Ch'ien Lung, c. 1790, European market. A chaste, formal design clearly reflects the classical style popular in the Western world during the late eighteenth century. The scene of a pillared pavillion in front of which small figures are gathered is executed in sepia and black. This is enclosed by a blue enamel and gilt border. Diam: 9¾" (24.8 cm).

Cup and saucer, Ch'ien Lung, c. 1790, English market. Two different circular European scenes, both popular at the time, with rivers and townhouses in sepia decorate this cup and saucer. Each object contains a sepia "Fitzhugh" border. OH (cup): 2⅝" (6.7 cm); Diam (saucer): 5⅝" (14.3 cm).

Cup and saucer, Chia Ch'ing, c. 1810, American market. This interesting late work of a Chinese decorator who copied a European prototype is in the taste of the Directoire period and closely resembles a Sèvres cup and saucer of 1807. The seated classical figures are drawn in brown on a lemon-colored ground. The borders and handle of the cup are in gilt. The saucer has a frieze of classical urns and ewers around a broad sloping rim. The deep saucer may have been used to cool and drink tea. *See* Cox, fig. 974. OH (cup): 2½" (6.4 cm); Diam (saucer): 5⅝" (14.3 cm).

69

70

71

Platter, Ch'ien Lung, c. 1785, Indian (English Colonial) market. A mahout or keeper/driver sitting atop a brown elephant is sketched in rose and green, and wears a red hat. The details of the landscape are painted in polychrome enamels. The background is a *bianco-sopra-bianco* ground of flowers and vines. The Italian term refers to the textual effect obtained by using a thick white enamel or glaze against a white ground and was first used to describe sixteenth-century tin-glazed ware made chiefly at Urbino and Faenza. This piece has been copied in what is referred to today as "Hong Kong" porcelain which is a whiter white than the antique. OL: 15″ (38.1 cm).

Plate, Ch'ien Lung, c. 1736, Dutch market. The "Parasol" design was one of the most popular of the eighteenth century. The Delft chamber of the Dutch East India Company commissioned Cornelius Pronk (or Pronck, 1691–1759) to make drawings which would serve the Chinese decorators as models. The design was copied by the Japanese around 1740 and the Venetian Cozzi factory c. 1765. The central scene is executed in underglaze blue. Details in *rouge de fer* and gilt heighten the blue. An elongated cell diaper border in *rouge de fer* and orange contains eight cartouches of four birds alternating with four figures. On the reverse of the rim are seven insects drawn in underglaze blue. The "Parasol" center design was usually painted in a circle rather than within a square as seen here. The design was also executed in underglaze blue, and in a rose red. Diam: 8⅝" (22 cm).

Teapoy, Ch'ien Lung, c. 1750, European market. The figure of the gentleman is often referred to as "Governor Duff." Actually this gentleman was known as Diederik Durven, Governor-General of the Dutch East India Company. It has been suggested, however, that the couple pictured might be Louis XIV and Madame de Maintenon. Most probably it is neither gentleman nor the famed French woman. The object is decorated in *rouge de fer* with gilt and some black. *See* Scheurleer, fig. 203. OH: 4⅞" (12.4 cm).

Bowl, Ch'ien Lung, c. 1760, European market. Two scenes of Chinese acrobats and jugglers in polychrome enamels, sepia, and black alternate with two sepia landscape panels. OH: 2½" (6.4 cm), Diam (top) 5½" (14 cm).

Plate, Ch'ien Lung, c. 1760, European market. A silver ground provides a brilliant setting for an interior scene with Chinese figures. The silvered ground color, now tarnished to a metallic black, is a very unusual addition to a typical Chinese *famille rose* genre scene. Difficulties in production and unsuccessful results limited the use of this technique. There are, however, a number of mid-eighteenth century porcelains with details and tracery in silver. The figures are drawn in polychrome enamels, *rouge de fer*, and gilt. Diam: 9¹⁵⁄₁₆" (25.3 cm).

74

75

76

Bowl (above), and saucer (below), Ch'ien Lung, c. 1770, European market. These designs may be considered prototypes of the nineteenth-century Rose Medallion and Mandarin porcelains exported from China to North America in great quantities. All the design is executed in polychrome enamels with gilt and *rouge de fer*. In the scene Chinese figures perform household tasks in a house and courtyard as two women ride past on horseback. OH (bowl): 2½″ (6.4 cm), Diam: 5½″ (14 cm); Diam (saucer): 6¹⁄₁₆″ (15.4 cm).

78   *From left,* miniature tea bowl and saucer, teapot, cup, and cream jug, Chia Ch'ing, c. 1805, English market. The scene of children playing leapfrog after school is derived from a painting by the English artist Thomas Stothard, R.A. (1755–1834). These are representative pieces from a set made for children, and each is drawn in polychrome enamel colors with sepia and black. The borders are in blue enamel and gilt. Another scene showing children leaving home for school was also used, and possibly both these were taken from French prints after the original paintings. OH (tea bowl): 1⅜" (3.5 cm), Diam (top): 2¼" (5.7 cm); Diam (saucer): 3¾" (9.5 cm); OH (teapot): 3¾" (9.5 cm), OW: 6⅝" (16.8 cm); OH (cup): 2⅛" (5.4 cm), Diam (top): 1⅞" (4.7 cm); OH (cream jug): 3⅜" (8.6 cm).

Punch bowl, Ch'ien Lung, c. 1780, European market. A view of the foreign hongs at the Chinese port of Canton is pictured on this bowl in polychrome enamels with *rouge de fer,* black, and sepia. Europeans were always interested in renderings of the wood and brick buildings which were used by foreign merchants as residences, offices, and warehouses. On the inside of the bowl's rim are hanging baskets with polychrome floral swags which extend from husk and fret bands. The inside bottom is decorated with a Chinese vase in *rouge de fer* and this is filled with polychrome enamel flowers. These flowers are surrounded by green enamel with a gilt husk border featuring polychrome floral sprays. OH: 5¹³⁄₁₆" (14.8 cm), Diam: 14" (35.6 cm).

77

VI. Blanc de Chine

Blanc de chine ware brought to the West in the late seventeenth and early eighteenth centuries is clearly identified by the smooth, creamy white to pure white glaze that unites with the body of the work. "In some cases," Joseph T. Butler has observed, "the vitrification is so complete that the piece resembles glass."[1] The objects made with this unique glaze at Tê-Hua in Ch'uan-Chou in southern Fukien province are not, however, completely without added decoration. Small spots of color embellish some of the animal figures, as seen in figure 79. Other forms were painted with opaque enamels; whether this process took place at Tê-Hua or was handled elsewhere is still a matter of some conjecture.

Production of this ware began sometime during the Sung dynasty (960–1279) and came to the attention of Dutch traders in the early seventeenth century. The factories at Ching-tê Chên were virtually out of operation by the mid-century and would remain closed—at least to Westerners—until 1683. To a large extent, *blanc de chine* from Tê-Hua took the place of more colorful enamelled ware on the outwardbound European ships. "By the 1680s," Clare Le Corbeiller has written, "Tê-Hua porcelain was well-known in Europe. . . . Its acceptability in the West was largely due to its unadorned whiteness that allowed of locally added painted decoration."[2] To identify such pieces today is extremely difficult. Only the nearly pure white objects made during the K'ang Hsi, Yung Chêng, and Ch'ien Lung can be documented with any sort of accuracy.

Figures of animals are among the forms sent to the West from the mid-seventeenth to the mid-eighteenth centuries. These are extremely charming, well-modelled objects, many of which may have been based on mythical Oriental creatures. Chinese potters did copy European animal forms; those of Tê-Hua, however, remain closer to traditional domestic models of considerable antiquity. A writer of nearly unquestioned authority, P. J. Donnelly, claims that only cockerels and parrots were made in *blanc de chine* specifically for the Western market.[3] If this is the case, then the figures of such animals as dogs produced for the export trade are more rare than anyone has yet surmised.

The most common of the subjects encountered in *blanc de chine* is that of the erroneously labelled "Governor Duf" group (plate XI). G. C. Williamson in *The Book of Famille Rose* (London, 1927), first identified the adult male figure in the group as one Governor Duf with his Chinese wife. No such person ever existed. In addition, the individual about whom Williamson became confused, most probably Diederick Durven, Dutch Governor General at Batavia from 1729 to 1732, never married a Chinese woman. The real story is both simpler and more obscure: the figures in European dress are without any real identity and stand merely as representative of Western types.

There are several variations of these figural groups, but the vast majority contain four persons—two men in European dress on the left and two women costumed in the Chinese manner on the right. The figure farthest to the left is variously identified as an attendant or a child, although, as Donnelly notes, European children did not wear periwigs.[4] He adds further that "Almost all these groups can be dated by their costume to the first quarter of the eighteenth century, and even where the costume is earlier the piece is not."[5] True Fukien figural groups of this sort can also be identified by the appearance of a central piece of Chinese furniture in front of which is placed a potted plant; before the gentlemen is found a dog; before the women is placed a monkey.

The Tê-Hua potters were also responsible for other types of figures and objects sent to the West. Some of the earliest are representations of the Chinese goddess Kuan-yin as well as other religious or mythological subjects. It is not surprising, therefore, that the Chinese should later turn to the production of markedly religious European pieces such as the Virgin and Child, Adam and Eve, and St. Anthony of Padua holding the infant Jesus. These may have been almost exact copies of European forms supplied by missionaries. The work of the Chinese was not always of the highest grade, but the glaze was usually of a much heavier consistency than that applied by European ceramists.

In addition to these religious wares there are also tea and coffee pots, mugs and cups, plates and dishes, and porringers. European metal forms were supplied for copying for traditional Western pieces. According to Donnelly, there are no known tea caddies, sweetmeat dishes or mustard pots. The wide assortment of ware made at Ching-tê Chên was clearly unknown at Tê-Hua. The export trade was important there, but it was not developed to the same degree in the latter place. Rather, the potters chose to work in a manner more closely allied to their native tradition. This approach is confirmed by the production of hundreds of thousands of miniature objects, most often toy whistles, in various human and animal forms.

NOTES

[1] Joseph T. Butler, "Chinese Porcelain Figures of Westerners," in *Chinese Export Porcelain*, ed. Elinor Gordon (New York: Universe Books, 1975), p. 90.

[2] Clare Le Corbeiller, *China Trade Porcelain: Patterns of Exchange* (New York: The Metropolitan Museum of Art, 1974), p. 23.

[3] P. J. Donnelly, *Blanc de Chine, The Porcelain of Tê-Hua in Fukien* (London: Faber and Faber, Ltd., 1969, and New York: Frederick A. Praeger, 1969), p. 205.

[4] *Ibid.*, p. 192.

[5] *Ibid.*, p. 205.

79

Figure of seated hound, Yung Chêng, c. 1730, European market; figure
of spaniel, Ch'ien Lung, c. 1760, European market. Although designed
and produced for Western customers, the figures of animals made at
Tê-hua of *blanc de chine* are unmistakably Oriental in form and composition. These are a far cry from the traditional figures, such as the
Dog of Fo or lionine forms widely used in domestic ceramics, sculpture,
and painting. Nevertheless, the *blanc de chine* animals were not modeled specifically on Western examples. They remained purely the province of Chinese ceramic specialists. Decorators, from Canton or elsewhere, rarely exercised their more colorful and Western talents on them.
The hound is marked only with iron brown eyes and a similarly colored
spot on its forehead. Other animal figures have patches of black and/or
brown. OH (seated hound): 7½″ (19.1 cm); OH (spaniel): 5⅞″ (14.9
cm), OL: 6¾″ (16.1 cm) .

VII. Animal Forms

Porcelain objects in animal forms are of special interest to collectors of export ware. To clearly identify and to trace the lineage of such pieces, however, is an exercise in patience and great skill. In no other area, perhaps, have European and Far Eastern forms and motifs become quite so intermixed. There is no doubt that Chinese ceramists borrowed ideas from their counterparts in England, France, Holland, and Germany; the contrary was also the case during the seventeenth and eighteenth centuries. Of the objects to be encountered, the figures are more clearly Chinese or Oriental in inspiration; objects of a more utilitarian form such as tureens or drinking cups are usually based on European models. In terms of modelling and decoration, the earlier Chinese export figures from the K'ang Hsi period are far superior to those produced at a later time. The Chinese potter as a copy artist of eighteenth-century Meissen and Chelsea wares, however, was a surprisingly inventive and talented workman.

Writers on the subject of export ware are rarely as candid or as helpful in their commentary as is Pamela C. Copeland in an article written for *Antiques*, "Oriental Porcelain Frivolities," in 1966. Mrs. Copeland expresses her love for figural objects which "appeal to me on account of their spontaneity, imagination, and whimsical humor."[1] She does not, however, hide the fact that mistakes in identifying Chinese-made objects have been made by herself, a skilled collector, or other experts. At the same time, she does not shirk the responsibility of making judgments. After discussing the close interrelationship between East and West, she states, "It has been said that the animal, bird, and figure forms are the outcome of this increasing contact with the Western world. Certainly, European taste affected the Chinese potter; nevertheless, many of these forms had been used by the Chinese for ages to represent the supernatural and mystical."[2] Representative of this kind of object is certainly the figure of a deer, c. 1720, illustrated in color, plate XIII. Other forms based on Chinese mythological sources are the Fêng-huang, mythical birds, figure 86, the *blanc de chine* hound and spaniel illustrated in figure 79, and the rhyton, figure 80.

Other animal forms with ancient roots in Chinese mythology and religion are the cocks and cockerels, birds of fame, and the elephant which, as Mrs. Copeland speculates, may have come to China from India with the introduction of Buddhism. The duck is another such traditional form and was used in early mythology as a symbol of marital happiness and fidelity. The ways in which these forms were executed, however, were determined in large extent by European practice. For instance, both the pug dog, figure 82, and the elephant, figure 87, are considered by many to have been fitted with candle-holders, and, indeed, these figures were intended to be used in this manner by Europeans. In Chinese practice, however, the holder was so shaped for the purpose of burning incense.

Much more clearly European in form and decoration is the figure of a parrot from the K'ang Hsi period, figure 81, which is probably a Delft copy. So, too, may be the parrot wall pockets, figure 88, of a much later date. Figures of cows, not illustrated here, were certainly first modelled on Dutch faience samples. The pug dog "candleholder" in *rouge de fer*, figure 82, is said to have been introduced by the master Meissen ceramic artist, Johann Joachim Kändler, about 1735, but he may have been following a Chinese form.[3] The pair of hound figures illustrated in color, plate XIV, present us with a similar dilemma. These were produced in both Germany and China. Only an examination of glazes by an expert will determine their origin for sure. Those illustrated here are known to be Chinese.

The Meissen and Chelsea factories were particularly proficient in producing exquisitely modelled and decorated assorted pieces for dinner settings such as tureens, salt dishes, mustard pots, etc. Kändler's two thousand and two hundred-piece Swan Service, 1737–1741, is the acknowledged masterpiece in such baroque porcelain. English and German potters turned to animal and vegetal forms to produce the kind of object seen in figure 81, a tureen in the form of a hawk, and, in figure 85, a covered dish in the remarkable shape of a dormouse. The Chinese did not embellish their ware to the degree indulged by the Europeans, but in such sculptural creations as the figure of a peacock, figure 83, and the birds in a natural setting, figure 84, they did attain a high degree of proficiency.

There is no doubt, as mentioned earlier, that export figural work in animal form was best executed in the K'ang Hsi and early Yung Chêng periods. Both modelers and decorators seem to have worked more imaginatively in more traditional forms. One can not, however, close one's eyes to the exceptional pieces which emerged at a later time. The figure of a mother and baby monkey, illustrated in color, plate XV, is just such an example. The figure is modelled with an expert sense of natural form, the glaze is smoothly applied, and the decoration is most aesthetically painted. The resemblance to a traditional Madonna and Child figurine is inescapable, but to speculate further about the origin of the design or the sculptor's intention, would be foolish. This piece presents the collector with the sobering knowledge that not all art from the past can be neatly categorized and explained.

NOTES

[1] Pamela C. Copeland, "Oriental Porcelain Frivolities," in *Chinese Export Porcelain*, ed. Elinor Gordon (New York: Universe Books, 1975), p. 61.

[2] *Ibid*.

[3] D. F. Lunsingh Scheurleer, *Chinese Export Porcelain* (London: Faber and Faber, Ltd., 1974, and New York: Pitman Publishing Corp., 1974), p. 174.

80

Rhyton, K'ang Hsi, c. 1710, European market. This very unusual form in Chinese porcelain is related to earlier T'ang dynasty models. Rhytons, cups or vessels with a handle in the form of an animal's horn, head, or entire body, were made as early as 500 B.C. in Greece in metal and ceramics. The water buffalo head is beautifully modeled and decorated in aubergine with black, large green eyes, and black horns around which is a yellow rope. OH: 4¾″ (12.1 cm).

81

Left, covered tureen in the form of a hawk, Ch'ien Lung, c. 1760, European market; *right,* figure of a parrot, K'ang Hsi, c. 1710, European market. The parrot is modeled and decorated in the same fine manner as the rhyton. The body is colored aubergine, green, and yellow with black details. The beak and talons are painted orange, and the figure is perched on a green and black rockwork base. The covered tureen is one of a pair, the upper body forming the removable cover. Rose breast feathers, polychrome enamel back feathers, and orange beak and talons constitute the decoration. OH (parrot): 7⅞″ (20 cm), OW: 5¼″ (13.3 cm); OL (covered tureen): 8″ (20.4 cm), OW: 4¾″ (12.2 cm).

82

Recumbent pug dog with incense holder, Ch'ien Lung, c. 1750-70, European market. The model for this figure, one of a pair, is originally Chinese. Only the Chinese would have modeled a dog in this manner. Copies of these were made by Chelsea, Bow, and Longton Hall, as well as Meissen. The animal is painted in *rouge de fer* with black eyes; the holder, used by the Chinese for incense and by Europeans for a candle, is decorated in polychrome enamels. OH: 3¾" (9.5 cm), OL: 6⅜" (16.2 cm).

83   Figure of peacock, Ch'ien Lung, c. 1750-75, European market. This
creature is closely identified with China, despite the fact that its natural
habitat is that of India and Ceylon. The peacock is a motif found
decorating many pieces of export ware, and was a popular figure with
Westerners. Here it is executed with a red breast, wings in various
shades of green, and raised tail feathers in green with blue eyes. It is
standing on a dark green flowering branch. OH: 6¾₆" (15.7 cm), OW:
4¼" (10.8 cm).

84

Figure of birds in natural setting, Ch'ien Lung, c. 1760, European market. This is a rare example of Chinese sculpture and one that is very realistically modeled. The birds, in lavender and black with rose feet and beaks, are perched on a grey/brown stump with pink flowers and leaves. OH: 7$\frac{1}{16}$" (18 cm), OW (base): 6$\frac{3}{8}$" (16.2 cm), OD: 5" (12.7 cm).

85

Covered dish in shape of dormouse, Ch'ien Lung, c. 1760, European market. A curious piece, this is one that might have limited appeal at the table. The cover finial, a baby dormouse, is a charming and clever device. Both mother and child are painted in brown. The adult feeds on grape-stones or berries and rests on a leaf-shaped base decorated, as is the lid, with scattered flowers in polychrome enamel colors and a single cell border in *rouge de fer* and black. *See* Beurdeley, cat. 100. OL: 9″ (22.9 cm), OW: 7½″ (19.1 cm).

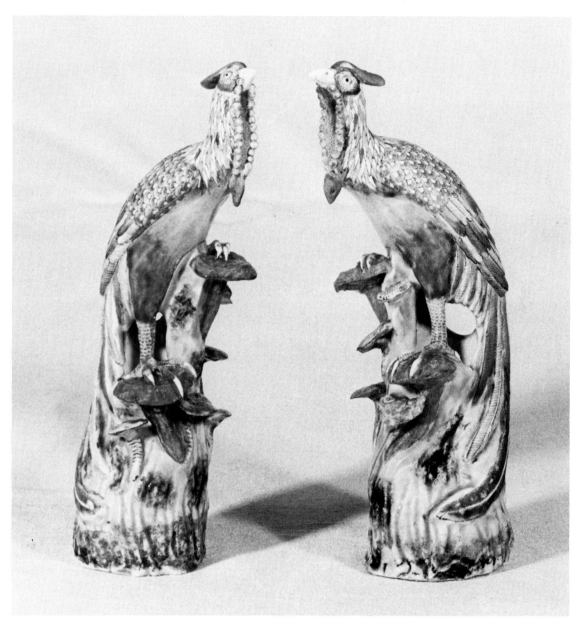

86

Pair of figures of phoenix "feng-hûang" birds, Ch'ien Lung, 1780-1820, European market. These phoenix birds, decorated in polychrome enamel colors, are perched on tall, pierced rockwork bases washed in green and black. The phoenix symbolizes the south point of the compass for the Chinese, and is a bisexual bird, "feng" being the male and "hûang" the female manifestation. It is the emblem of the Empress and has the head of a pheasant, the beak of a swallow, a long flexible neck, and the tail of a peacock. OH (largest): $7^{15}\!/_{16}$" (20.2 cm).

87 Figure of elephant supporting an incense holder, Ch'ia Ching, c. 1800, English or American market. This red-orange elephant, clothed in covers of brown, rose, green, and gilt, supports a holder decorated with green and rose flowers. Westerners used this holder for a candle. OH: 7½″ (19.1 cm), OL: 8¾″ (22.3 cm).

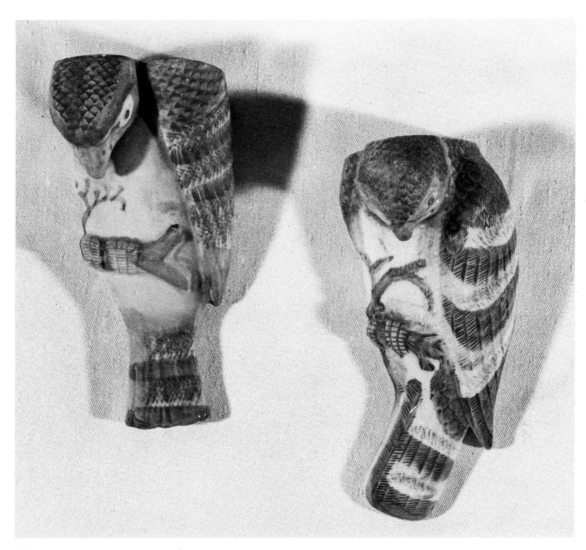

88

Pair of parrot-form wall pocket flower holders, Chia Ch'ing, c. 1800, English or American market. The pockets are decorated in underglaze blue. OL (largest): 8″ (20.4 cm).

VIII. Assorted Forms

Collectors of porcelain of all countries and times are always delighted by the assorted wares which depart from customary form. The long procession of plates, platters, soup bowls, etc., can become a somewhat tedious path to follow if it is not broken with the introduction of the odd and curious and the one-of-a-kind. By the eighteenth century, Chinese potters were particularly adept at producing special wares for their foreign customers. Some of these were not at all unusual for their time, but now strike us as being, if not singular, then at least novel. Many of these objects must have been produced as special orders. Almost all are based on European forms and probably were adapted from porcelain, pewter, or silver models brought by traders as early as the seventeenth century.

Typical of the objects copied from silver are the ladle bowls illustrated in figures 104 and 105. The cane handle, figure 89, is clearly an imitation of similar forms made at Meissen, Chantilly, and St. Cloud, c. 1725–1750. Other traditional European porcelain forms are those of the bough pot, watch case, bordaloue, mug, eye cup, candlesticks, covered dish, tureen, and lid inserts and tiles. This, by no means, exhausts the list of forms which could be enumerated. As was discussed in the section on animal figures, Oriental and Western expression in porcelain during the late seventeenth and eighteenth centuries was in a constant state of flux, decorated objects being exchanged across long distances. This interchange of techniques and forms quickened in pace as world trade in porcelain continued to grow between East and West. Today even the acknowledged expert in world porcelain types may encounter difficulty in differentiating a Meissen model from its Chinese copy and vice versa.

The Chinese decorator's attempts to capture European genre scenes is documented in the series of four lid inserts, figures 91 through 94. Surely considered decadent by Chinese standards, these harmless vignettes of European-style licentiousness are rendered in a naïve and amusing manner. How accurate they are as copies is impossible to determine since the originals are not available for examination, but it does seem that the Chinese painter lost none of the voluptuous line or detail that must have defined the European drawings.

Other objects illustrate even more clearly the Chinese potter's ability to successfully copy European forms and decorative techniques. Porcelain handles for silverware, figure 98, were made to fit European metal. It should be noted, however, that the Chinese also used such porcelain pieces for their own export metal flatware made of paktong, an alloy of copper, nickel, and zinc. The covered dish in the form of a wooden shoe or *sabot* is a form that derives from France. The mug shaped in the image of Bacchus (identified as Neptune by some other writers), figure 106, is based on a Chelsea-Derby original introduced in 1778. Chelsea is also the source for the design of the watch case, figure 100. The bordaloue or portable chamber pot, figure 101, owes its inspiration to some very practical-minded French potter.

Hundreds of other objects could be illustrated here, and each would tell the reader something of the complex nature of the trade between East and West in the 1700s. Porcelain plaques and tiles, chandeliers, torchères, stem cups based on Dutch and English drinking glasses, spittoons, butter dishes, wine cups, ewers, casters, ink pots, barber's basins—all these and many more were produced at Ching-tê Chên, decorated there or in Canton, and shipped to Europe and North America. Only when European ceramic production began to match that of the Chinese in price and quantity during the last half of the eighteenth century did this flow of imitative wares begin to slow.

European porcelain makers could not, however, always duplicate the brilliant decoration or fineness of paste or glaze achieved by their Chinese counterparts. An object such as the eggplant tureen, figure 97, was formed and painted in as fine a manner as any porcelain of the time. Other tureens made in China based on European models display the same sort of exceptional workmanship.[1] The same might be said for the candlesticks, figure 96, decorated in the Imari fashion. Chinese decorators adapted the Japanese style of painting in *rouge de fer*, gilt, and underglaze blue for export ware at least as early as 1716.[2] The decorators at Delft also appropriated the Imari design, but the more delicate Chinese wares are clearly recognizable.

Of all the assorted forms, that of the garniture set, as illustrated in color (plate XII), is most markedly Chinese. These were used originally in a reception area or were placed on an altar. Makers of Delft faience began to produce such objects in the seventeenth century and by c. 1726 they were also being made at Meissen.[3] Usually comprised of five vases—three jars and two beakers—they became known in Europe as *garniture de cheminée*, and were most often used to decorate mantels or cupboards. Sets of three and seven are also known to have been made. Their popularity in the West continued well into the nineteenth century, and the quality of design suffered with the advance of time. The delicate *famille rose* motif of mid-eighteenth-century ware was eventually superseded by Rose Medallion and Mandarin designs of a somewhat gaudy and heavy sort.

NOTES

[1] See Michel Beurdeley, *Chinese Trade Porcelain* (Rutland, Vermont: Charles E. Tuttle Co., 1962), p. 45, and Arlene M. Palmer, *A Winterthur Guide to Chinese Export Porcelain* (New York: Crown Publishers, 1976), pp. 51, 57.

[2] D. F. Lunsingh Scheurleer, *Chinese Export Porcelain* (London: Faber and Faber, Ltd., 1974, and New York: Pitman Publishing Corp., 1974, p. 165.

[3] *Ibid.*, p. 88.

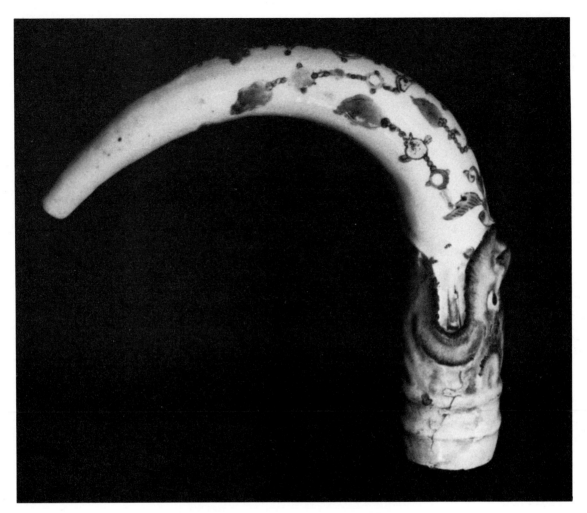

89

Handle for cane or walking stick, Ch'ien
Lung, c. 1740, European market. The
head of a lion or dog, in *rouge de fer*, at
the base of this handle seems to hold in
its mouth a necklace of flowers and jewels
in polychrome enamels. OW: 4¾" (12.1
cm), OH: 4" (10.2 cm).

90

Left, water dropper, Ch'ien Lung, c. 1740, European market; *right,* spoon, Ch'ien Lung, c. 1760, European market. The popular Lotus pattern is used in both these items. Rose, green, and blue enamels form the decoration. The stem (handle) of the water dropper is in olive green enamel. The hollow handle opens into the bowl near its bottom allowing water to flow out of the handle in drops. The water dropper was used by Chinese scholars writing with a brush. OL (water dropper): 6⅜₁₆" (15.7 cm); OL (spoon): 7¼" (18.4 cm).

91- 94

Four lid inserts, Ch'ien Lung, c. 1750, European market. Each of the four inserts has an amorous scene painted on one side with a small scene of birds set in landscapes on the reverse. All the decoration is in black. When used as lids the more adventuresome scenes were to be affixed inside small boxes with the conventional Chinese scenes facing out. OL (varies in size): 3″ to 3⅛″ (7.6 to 7.9 cm), OH (varies in size): from 2¼″ to 2⅜″ (5.7 to 6.1 cm).

Eye cup, Ch'ien Lung, c. 1750, European market. This eye cup, a rare form in Chinese export ware, is decorated with polychrome enamel flowers. A gilt cup and ball border is painted in the interior. OH: 2⁵⁄₁₆″ (5.9 cm).

Pair of candlesticks, Ch'ien Lung, c. 1750, European market. This pair of candlesticks, modeled after a European metal form, are decorated in underglaze blue, *rouge de fer*, and gilt in the popular Imari style. OH (both): 6¼″ (15.8 cm).

95

96

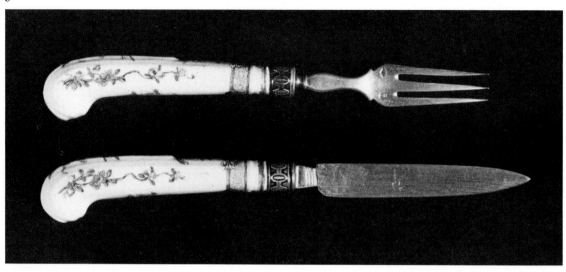

Knife and fork, Ch'ien Lung, c. 1760, European market. Silver utensils signed "E. PETER" are fitted with porcelain handles. These are decorated with flowers in polychrome enamel colors. OL (knife): 7⁷⁄₁₆″ (18.9 cm); OL (fork): 6¾″ (17.1 cm).

Small covered tureen and stand, Ch'ien Lung, c. 1760, European market. Tureens of this sort were often modeled on naturalistic forms popular in Europe. Objects of this sort in the shape of a peach or melon are known to have been made. This very rare tureen is in the form of an eggplant. It is decorated with an aubergine glaze and has a leaf-shaped cover. The finial of the cover is a small modeled insect in green and *rouge de fer*. The stand is decorated with the "Tobacco Leaf" pattern. OH: 3¾″ (9.5 cm), OL: 8¾″ (22.3 cm).

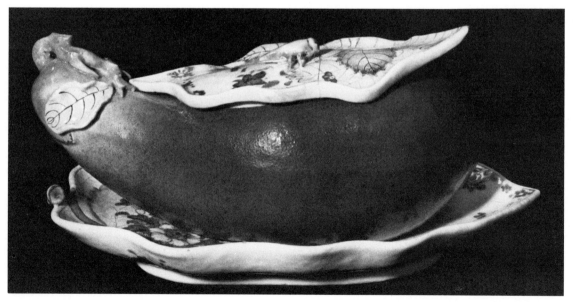

97

99

Bough pot, Ch'ien Lung, c. 1760, European market. A holder for floral branches was probably modeled after a European porcelain prototype. It is decorated with polychrome enamel colors with gilt borders and handles. OH: 7¼" (18.4 cm), OW: 7" (17.8 cm).

100

Watch case, Ch'ien Lung, c. 1760, European market.
This case is decorated in a somewhat simpler manner
than other such forms made for export. The decoration, however, does reflect the influence of English
Chelsea wares. The flowers and vines are applied and
painted in polychrome enamel colors and gilt. The
finial is a small jardiniere filled with flowers. Gilt
floral bands surround the lid and the top of the base.
OH: 7⅝″ (19.4 cm).

101

Bordaloue, Ch'ien Lung, c. 1760, European market. One of the most practical objects made for export, the bordaloue derives its name from Louis Bordaloue (1632–1704), a celebrated and long-winded French Jesuit preacher. The object is decorated with floral sprays in polychrome enamels and gilt spear borders. OL: 10¼″ (26 cm), OW: 4¾″ (12.1 cm).

102

Covered dish in the form of a sabot, Ch'ien
Lung, c. 1760, French market. Containers modeled in the shape of a wooden shoe are found
in several forms, some fitted with silver lids.
This covered dish is decorated with polychrome
enamel flowers, gilt details, and underglaze blue
cell diaper borders. A miniature sabot is the
finial. The floral sprays are painted in a particularly delicate way and are characteristic of
the French taste in export ware. Beurdeley (cat.
108) has catalogued a sweetmeat dish in the
form of a lady's high-heeled slipper. OL: 7¼"
(18.5 cm).

Plate XI. *The Game Players,* K'ang Hsi, c. 1700, Dutch market. This figure group is worked in *blanc de chine,* a porcelain chiefly made at Tê-Hua in southern Fukien province. Glazes range from creamy white in the earliest Sung wares to a purer white by the K'ang Hsi reign, and seem to melt into the surface of the body. The European gentleman and Chinese lady are seated at a gameboard with their attendants (or children). Figure groups such as this one are often referred to as "Governor Duff" groups, thought by some to be Diederick Durven (1676–1740), Dutch Governor General at Batavia from 1729–1732, and his Chinese wife. Durven has often been confused with Hendrik Doeff, director of the Dutch East India Company factory in Japan during the early nineteenth century. OH: 5⅝" (14.3 cm), OW: 5⅞" (14.9 cm), OD: 3⅛" (7.9 cm).

Plate XII. Five-piece mantel garniture, Ch'ien Lung, c. 1750, European market. The "garniture de cheminée" were made as early as the Yung Chêng dynasty (1723–1735) to decorate mantels and cabinets, and were even displayed in the fireplace during warm months. This rare five-piece set is decorated with polychrome enamel tree peonies in reserves on a brilliant rose ground, with borders of lotus blossoms growing from curling, stylized green stems. OH (beaker vases): 9½" (24.2 cm), OH (covered vases): 11¼" (28.6 cm).

Plate XIII. Figure of deer, K'ang Hsi, c. 1720, Dutch market. An extremely unusual piece, this early figure is decorated in a manner reminiscent of Ch'êng Hua (1465–1487) painting. Figures of this sort were usually decorated in a naturalistic fashion or left completely white. All the decoration here is underglaze blue. This figure has been exhibited at the Metropolitan Museum. OH: 10¼″ (26 cm), OL: 8¼″ (21 cm).

Plate XIV. Pair of hound figures, Ch'ien Lung, c. 1750–1775, European market. The bodies of these two animal figures are extremely well formed and colored, their tails being wrapped into the contours shaped by the hind legs. The fancy collars are of gilt and green while the bodies themselves are naturalistically shaded in *rouge de fer* and white. *See* Hyde, pl. XII and Phillips, pl. 73. OH (tallest): 9¾″ (24.8 cm).

Plate XV. Figure of mother and baby monkey, Tao Kuang, c. 1830, European market. Although a late piece of export ware, this figure is extremely well modeled and colored. The blue, green, yellow, and brown enamels have been applied with an eye to naturalistic and aesthetic effects. OH: $10^{15}/_{16}''$ (27.8 cm).

103

Pair of covered jars, Ch'ien Lung, c. 1770, European market. The elaborate design used on these containers may have been inspired by the Meissen "schneeball" (snowball) decoration developed by Johann Joachim Kändler in the mid-eighteenth century—a covering of applied small white flowers. The jars are completely surrounded with single flower petals and several full flowers and leaves. The overall glaze is in a turquoise color. OH (largest, *left*): 3⅞" (9.8 cm).

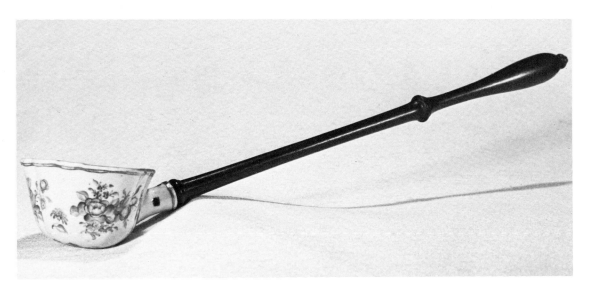

Ladle, Ch'ien Lung, c. 1760–1800, American or European market. The ladle bowls were copied from traditional Western silver models and were produced over a number of years beginning in about 1760. The flowers on the bowl of this ladle are rendered in rose enamel. Gilt edges band the bowl and extension. OL (with handle): 14⅜″ (41.7 cm), OL (bowl): 3⅞″ (9.8 cm).

Ladle, Ch'ien Lung, 1760–1800, American or European market. Flowers in polychrome enamels decorate this very similar ladle. OL (with handle): 12⅜″ (31.5 cm), OL (bowl): 3⅞″ (9.8 cm).

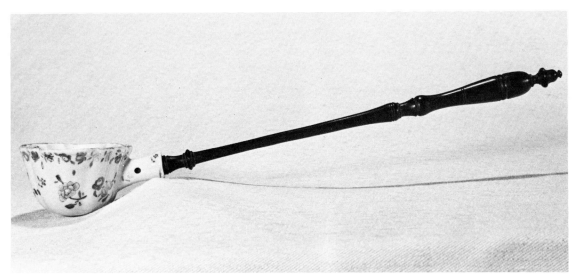

105

106

Mug, Ch'ien Lung, c. 1785, European market. A head of Bacchus has been modeled in the form of a mug. It is a copy of an English Chelsea-Derby original introduced in 1778. A very similar mug with the head of Jupiter was also copied by the Chinese from the English porcelain original. The Bacchus head is decorated in brown, flesh tones, and *rouge de fer*, and is crowned with a green and mulberry enamel grape vine. OH: 3⅞" (9.8 cm), OW: 5" (12.7 cm).

107

Set of nine nested bowls, Chia Ch'ing, c. 1810, American or European market. The thick enamel painting and exceedingly crowded Rose Medallion pattern stand in marked contrast to the delicate eighteenth-century chinoiserie designs in *famille rose* enamels. The typical Rose Medallion pattern as seen here is characterized by scrolled panels of floral groups alternating with similar panels of Mandarin scenes in polychrome enamels. These elements are painted on a ground of rose flowers and green vines with gilding in the background. OH (largest bowl): 2⅜" (6.1 cm), Diam (top): 4⁵⁄₁₆" (10.95 cm); OH (smallest bowl): ⅞" (2.2 cm), Diam (top): 2¼" (5.7 cm).

IX. "Fitzhugh" Decoration

Porcelain painted with the several variants of the "Fitzhugh" pattern have been a source of considerable mystery to scholars in the field for many years. The term itself is one that has gained widespread currency only in America, although, as will be explained, it is a name which most probably derives from England. Simply, "Fitzhugh" refers to a pattern consisting of a central medallion, four surrounding panels of floral design representing aspects of the Chinese arts, and a repeating border design of diapering, butterflies, flowers, trellis, and a Greek key fret. An inner cell diaper border is also often used. The central medallion is sometimes replaced by eagles, initials, or coats-of-arms. The design occurs most commonly in underglaze blue but was produced as well in orange, green, sepia, mulberry, yellow, black, and in combinations of two colors. The pattern became extremely popular in the 1780s and '90s and remained in use into the 1800s, especially in America. Some objects contain only the "Fitzhugh" border and these are not classified as being of this type.

Why, then, all the confusion? First, there is the problem of the term. None of the terms employed by Westerners were used by the Chinese themselves; they are convenient labels which have gained respectability with age. Of these, however, only "Fitzhugh" is without substantive descriptive meaning. *Blanc de chine, famille rose, famille verte*—these say something of the decorative process or lack thereof. In addition, ware termed "Fitzhugh" is terribly difficult to document. Being of a late variety, the objects are rarely of the custom-made sort ordered by Europeans, and since only a small amount of such ware was received in Europe, scholars there have not attempted to properly classify it. Their attitude, not without some merit, is summed up succinctly by one such expert: "Although it is authentic, porcelain of this late period is of no interest to the collector."[1]

To the American collector it is of extreme interest. For all serious collectors, an understanding of the development of the "Fitzhugh" pattern helps to explain much of the changing nature of the China trade at the end of the eighteenth and beginning of the nineteenth centuries. It is our belief that the appearance of the "Fitzhugh" pattern provides the link between European and American export ware, a not insignificant chapter in decorative history. And although many of these porcelains are markedly inferior in quality to those of the early and mid-eighteenth century, a substantial number do exhibit a high level of craftsmanship.

What, then, can be made of the term itself? Sir Algernon Tudor-Craig, a most reputable scholar in every other respect, confused things in his monumental *Armorial Porcelain of the Eighteenth Century* (London, 1925), and stuck to his badly-loaded guns in a 1930 article for *Antiques* magazine. In his own words, "Last, but not least in interest, we find, about 1800, the Fitzhugh pattern, so called in America only, owing to the fact that an old sea captain, trading from Salem, Massachusetts, to China, used to buy large consignments of this porcelain at Foochow and return with it to his home port for his wife to sell during his next trip. She, dear lady, apparently did not hold with such outlandish names; so Foochow became Fitzhugh and thus remains to this day."[2]

Most unlikely! "Foochow" is quite a jump from "Fitzhugh," even for a Salem lady. The Chinese port of this name was not opened to Western traders until 1840, many years after "Fitzhugh" had declined in popularity. Much more plausible is the story told thirty-six years later by J. B. S. Holmes, also in *Antiques*.[3] Briefly, an English trading family by the name of FitzHugh had been involved in the China trade since the early eighteenth century. Captain William FitzHugh first sailed to China in 1703 and one of his sons, Thomas, served the British East India Company in several positions, the last as president of the Canton factory from 1779–1781. Thomas, his son, Thomas II, and a nephew, William FitzHugh, were responsible for sending thousands of porcelain objects back to England. Among the prized possessions inherited by members of the family and proudly displayed as late as the 1960s is a blue and white platter of "Fitzhugh" design. Family members had never heard of the pattern before this time, but this is not surprising since the term, as Sir Tudor-Craig correctly states, has not been used in Great Britain or the Continent. Whether the FitzHugh family originally possessed other objects decorated in this manner is not known, but documented pieces with the traditional border were sent to England in the last quarter of the eighteenth century. According to D. F. Lansingh Scheurleer, "It occurs in pieces for the English and the American markets in the last thirty to thirty-five years of the eighteenth century, and the beginning of the nineteenth, and from time to time one comes across it on blue-and-white dinner services exported to the Netherlands. . . . In England, the Fitzhugh pattern was painted, among others, on Derby ware of c. 1770."[4]

It does not take too much imagination to suggest, as does Holmes, that American traders, reaching Canton for the first time in the 1780s, were introduced to English market ware that had been ordered by the FitzHugh family traders with this particular decoration. George Washington's Order of the Cincinnati service, one of the earliest brought from China, contains a "Fitzhugh" border in underglaze blue, figure 112. The border is identical to that seen in a covered oval tureen made for the Dutch or English markets in the late 1700s. That the central "Fitzhugh" decoration with separate groups of flowers and emblems surrounded by a medallion or monogram was also used at this time is evidenced by the presence of the FitzHugh family piece. Others will be uncovered in time, and a better chronology of the development of this stylistic change will emerge.

Post-Revolutionary Americans were not in the market for British porcelains, and turned to the Chinese to serve their porcelain needs. By the beginning of the nineteenth century, a large quantity of "Fitzhugh" had reached New York, Salem, Boston, Philadelphia, and other port cities. The majority of this ware was decorated in underglaze blue, and it is possible that this type was that first produced by the Chinese at Ching-tê Chên. As noted before, the underglaze blue border had made its appearance many years earlier. In addition to ornamenting Cincinnati porcelains, it was also used on early Canton with the now-familiar willow-tree pattern. It was not long, however, before there was a demand for more colorful ware. Some of these different single shades and combinations are illustrated in color, plate IX. Among them are some of the most rare colors, yellow, blue and gilt, green and orange, and brown and green. The blue plate illustrates yet another variation on the "Fitzhugh" designed ware—the use of a lattice and spear-head border usually found on Nanking.

Each of the "Fitzhugh" objects seen in the black and white figures, 108 through 111, dates from c. 1800. Three of these are illustrative of the many forms produced at the time for American and English customers. Whole services were, of course, produced for at least the American market. The platter, figure 111, which substitutes the usual central medallion with the American eagle, is typical of the finer wares sent to the New World. Those in various color combinations are also of special value today.

NOTES

1 Michel Beurdeley, *Chinese Trade Porcelain* (Rutland, Vermont: Charles E. Tuttle Co., 1962), p. 28.

2 Sir Algernon Tudor-Craig, "Chinese Armorial Porcelain, Some Eighteenth-Century Borders," *Chinese Export Porcelain*, ed. Elinor Gordon (New York: Universe Books, 1975), p. 149.

3 J. B. S. Holmes, "Fitzhugh and FitzHughs in the China Trade," *Chinese Export Porcelain*, ed. Elinor Gordon (New York: Universe Books, 1975), pp. 155–56.

4 D. F. Lunsingh Scheurleer, *Chinese Export Porcelain* (London: Faber and Faber, Ltd., 1974, and New York: Pitman Publishing Corp., 1974), pp. 132–33.

5 *Ibid.*, plate 163.

Garden seat, Chia Ch'ing, c. 1800, American or English market. Around the center of this seat, decorated in green, the four floral panels and central medallion of the "Fitzhugh" pattern are repeated twice. The panels alternate with two devices composed of Chinese coins and bowknots. The top and bottom borders are series of smaller repeats of the pattern. Garden or barrel-shaped seats were produced at least as early as the Sung dynasty. Termed a *liang tun* (cool seat), the form is based on that of an ancient drum. OH: 18½" (48.1 cm), OW (top): 10" (25.4 cm).

Covered tureen, Chia Ch'ing, c. 1800, American or English market. Sepia is the color used to draw the characteristic elements of the "Fitzhugh" pattern—medallion, floral panels, cell diaper border, and butterfly and trellis border. OH: 9¾" (24.8 cm), OW: 13¼" (33.7 cm).

108

Tea bowl, Chia Ch'ing, c. 1800, American or English market. The exterior of the bowl is decorated with the butterfly and trellis border and four usual floral panels. These are drawn in brown on a tan ground. A single cell border is found at the base and a cell diaper border is painted around the interior rim. OH: 2⅛″ (5.4 cm), Diam (top): 4¼″ (10.5 cm).

Platter, Chia Ch'ing, c. 1800, American market. An American eagle in sepia has been substituted for the central medallion of this very rare "Fitzhugh" piece in orange enamel with butterfly and trellis border. *See* also Mudge, figs. 63 and 90. 18½″ (47 cm) x 15¾″ (40 cm).

110

111

X. Order of the Society of Cincinnati China

The true treasures in Chinese export ware for the American market are those made for members of the Society of the Cincinnati at the end of the eighteenth century. This is a judgment reached by the majority of scholars on aesthetic grounds alone; that such objects are also of great historical value adds only to their luster. Examples of Cincinnati-decorated porcelain do appear from time to time on the market, but so rare have they become almost two hundred years after their creation that they are considered almost priceless. Even nearly forty years ago Homer Eaton Keyes reported that "various ambitious folk have endeavored to enlarge the visible supply by classifying in the Cincinnati category all porcelain showing the figure of a winged Fame or Victory. The absurdity of such a procedure should be patent. Cincinnati porcelain may occur without this figure . . . but *it may not occur without the emblem of the Society* [italics are the author's own]."[1]

The Society was formed in 1783 and included American and French officers of the Revolutionary War. The Society took its name from the legendary Roman senator Lucius Quinctius Cincinnatus, of the fifth century B.C., who left his farm for battle and returned there when his military duties were finished. On the death of a member, he is succeeded by his eldest son or other male heir under the law of primo-geniture. In recent years the rule has been changed to allow direct female descendants to succeed their fathers if there is no succeeding male. This hereditary form of succession aroused the opposition of many politicians at the time, especially those not eligible for membership. Of the 2,000 original members, George Washington was, of course, the most important and served as first president-general of the Order. Among the most important tasks to be undertaken was the designing of an armorial emblem. As Keyes notes, "the founders of the Society failed to realize that a really adequate fulfillment of their grandiloquent notions would necessitate a medal almost as large as a dish pan,"[2] but Major Pierre Charles L'Enfant was able to design a suitable medal in the form of a stately bald eagle with the addition of laurel and oak leaves. This medal is suspended from a deep blue ribbon two inches in width. A scene showing Cincinnatus receiving a sword and "other military ensigns" from three senators is shown on the obverse of the model; the reverse carries a rising sun, a city with open gates, vessels entering a port, and, in the foreground, Fame crowning Cincinnatus with a wreath inscribed *Virtutis Praemium*.

Samuel Shaw, aide-de-camp to General Henry Knox, was named secretary of the committee of officers which formed the Society. In 1784 he was chosen for the post of supercargo or business manager on the *Empress of China*, the first American ship to sail for China. A record of his service then and in the following years as the first American consul in China exists today in his journals edited by Josiah Quincy. We can read there of his first attempts to arrange the decoration of Cincinnati-design porcelain. Shaw worked with the

Canton enamelers in 1784 in executing a design suitable for members of the Society. It was meant to include, in Shaw's words, "the American Cincinnatus, under the conduct of Minerva, regarding Fame, who, having received from them the emblem of the order, was proclaiming it to the world." It was a miracle that the Chinese could make any sense out of this allegorical conception. Shaw reported that "The best of his [the decorator's] essays I preserved as a specimen of Chinese excellence in design and it is difficult to regard it without smiling."[3] The likeness was, indeed, excellent.

The service owned by Washington, unique in picturing a single figure of Fame with the insignia (figure 112 and plate XVII), must date from shortly after Shaw's initial attempts at art direction. He returned to America on the *Empress of China* in the spring of 1785 but his partner, Thomas Randall, remained to charter another ship and to bring back more cargo. Randall returned in August of the same year on the *Pallas* and evidently had been successful in continuing Shaw's earliest attempts to secure a Cincinnati design.

On August 12, 1785, the *Baltimore Advertiser* announced the imminent arrival of the *Pallas* with a valuable cargo which included Chinese porcelain: "Table-Sets of the best Nankin blue and white Stone China . . . Evening blue and white Stone China Cups and Saucers; Ditto painted; Ditto with the Arms of the Order of Cincinnati. . . ."[4] Although this advertisement does not specifically mention a large dinner service decorated with the Cincinnati emblem, George Washington wrote to Colonel Tench Tilghman, a former military aide then in business in Baltimore, "If great bargains are to be had, I would supply myself agreeably to an enclosed list," which included a full set of porcelain "With the badge of the Society of the Cincinnati if to be had."[5] Colonel Tilghman died in early 1786 without having obtained the porcelain, but on July 3, 1786, Colonel Henry "Light-Horse Harry" Lee, a delegate to the Continental Congress then sitting in New York, wrote Washington that a set could be purchased for approximately $150.

General Washington wrote Lee on July 26 to authorize the purchase. A receipted bill in Lee's name, dated August 7, 1786, shows that the set numbered 302 pieces. In Ledger B, Washington recorded: "In 1786 . . . Aug. 23 by 32 Guineas & ¼ of Moidore (a Portuguese coin) sent to Colo Henry Lee at New York, by Colo Humphreys to pay for a set of China bot. for me there . . . £ 45.5.0." The receipt of the porcelain was acknowledged by October 31 "without much damage."[6]

There is no firm evidence that this set was from the cargo of the *Pallas*, offered for sale in New York after failing to sell at Baltimore, but the *Pallas* was the only other ship besides the *Empress of China* to have returned to America before Washington purchased his service.

This first sale was the last difficult one to consummate. Other sets of Cincinnati ware, produced in the following years, quickly found owners. Keyes understood the reason for this: "Here, in short, arose the opportunity for American citizens to own armorial china, handsome and exclusive enough to compare favorably with the services which graced the tables of the aristocracy of Europe. Little time was lost in procuring a supply."[7]

Shaw had several tea and dinner services made for himself and for his friends (figures 113, 114, 115, 116, and plate XVIII). These sets are nearly identical in execution except for the individual initials. They include those of General Henry Knox, William Eustis (who also owned a second set), David Townsend (the Townsend tea set is now found at Historic Deerfield, Massachusetts), General Benjamin Lincoln, and James Jackson.

The Shaw cup and saucer (plate XVIII) are probably from a dinner service made between 1786 and 1788 while he was serving as consul in Canton. During his next stay, 1790 to 1792, he seems to have ordered the tea services made and sent to his friends in the Society.

NOTES

[1] Homer Eaton Keyes, "The Cincinnati and Their Porcelain," *Chinese Export Porcelain*, ed. Elinor Gordon (New York: Universe Books, 1975), p. 137.

[2] *Ibid.*, p. 134.

[3] Josiah Quincy, *The Journals of Major Samuel Shaw, The First Consul at Canton* (Boston, 1847), pp. 198–99.

[4] Keyes, p. 136.

[5] *Ibid.*

[6] *Ibid.*

[7] *Ibid.*, p. 135.

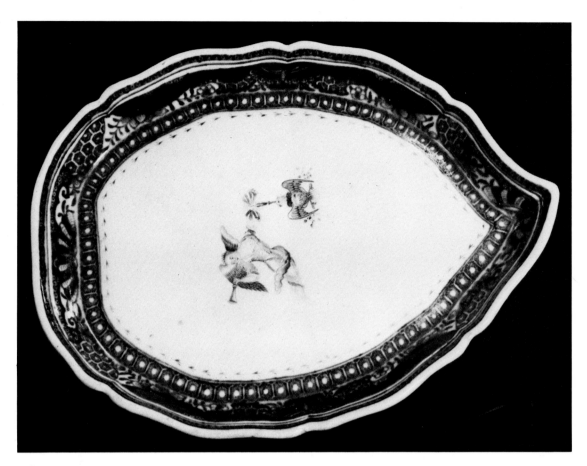

112

Leaf-shaped dish, Ch'ien Lung, c. 1784–85, American market. The service owned by George Washington is probably unique, as mentioned earlier, in the fact that the figure of "Fame" with the insignia is presented in single and not twin form. The so-called Henry "Light-Horse-Harry" Lee service may have been similarly decorated, but this has never been properly documented. Here the figure is seen dressed in light green and rose with sepia wings. It is trumpeting and holding the blue ribbon from which is suspended the society's insignia. The eagle of this medal is painted in gilt, as is a husk inner border. The cell diaper border and "Fitzhugh" outer border are decorated in underglaze blue. There are traces of gilt left at the edge of the piece. OL: 7⅝" (19.4 cm), OW: 5¾" (14.6 cm).

113

Covered cider jug, Ch'ien Lung, c. 1786–88, American market. The insignia of this jug is particularly well painted and preserved. Floral sprigs decorate the four corners and the cover. A finial in the shape of a Fo dog provides a handle for the cover. The view visible on the jug is that of Fame crowning Cincinnatus with a wreath; on the reverse side of the object is a scene showing Cincinnatus receiving a sword from three Roman senators. The eagle is drawn in sepia with white head and tail; the wreath surrounding his head is painted in green with red berries, and is held above by a blue ribbon. The gilt monogram *SS* stands for Samuel Shaw. A similar design appears on tea sets ordered by Shaw and sent by him to such friends as David Townsend, William Eustis, and General Henry Knox. OH: 9⅛″ (23.2 cm), Length from spout to handle: 7½″ (19.1 cm).

Above, teapot; *below*, teapot stand, Ch'ien Lung, c. 1790, American market. Polychrome enamels are used to decorate these Cincinnati pieces which are similar in many respects to the Shaw jug. The gilt monogram *WE* stands for William Eustis (1753–1825), Revolutionary War surgeon and vice-president of the Society of the Cincinnati from 1786 to 1810. The majority of this tea service is now to be found in the Diplomatic Reception Rooms of the State Department, Washington, D.C. OH (teapot): 5¼″ (13.3 cm); Diam (stand): 6½″ (16.5 cm).

116

Tray, Ch'ien Lung, c. 1795, American market. Twin angels are drawn in flesh tones with rose-colored scarves and brown wings. This piece is from a second service owned by William Eustis, the only known person to have two different Cincinnati services. Each of the angels holds a gilt trumpet in one hand and in the other the blue ribbon from which is suspended the Cincinnati insignia. This is painted in gilt with a green wreath. The borders are in gilt and blue enamel. 7⅛" (18.1 cm) x 5⅞" (14.9 cm).

Plate XVI. Platter with cover, Ch'ien Lung, c. 1765, cipher added, 1796–1810, American market. The use of landscape scenes in soft *famille rose* colors and gold spear borders mark these as pieces having an earlier life than that given them by "DWMC"—DeWitt Clinton (1769–1824) and his wife, Maria Franklin. Clinton, known best as Mayor of New York, Governor of New York State, and presidential candidate, married Maria Franklin in 1796. The service of which this platter is a part could have been held in the stock of an English or American merchant for some years, the cipher having been added at the later date. The figures of the Eight Taoist Immortals appear on the border of the platter and its cover. *See* Mudge, fig. 118 and Palmer, fig. 83. OL (platter): 20¾″ (52.8 cm), OW: 18⅛″ (46 cm). OL (cover): 16″ (40.7 cm), OH: 7″ (17.8 cm).

Plate XVII. Covered tureen, Ch'ien Lung, c. 1784–5, American market. George Washington purchased a dinner service of 302 pieces in 1786 and this tureen was among the items. Whether it was brought to the United States on the "Pallas," the second ship to return from China, is still a matter of conjecture. All of the Washington service is decorated with the insignia of the Society of the Cincinnati. On each side of the base of the tureen is the figure of Fame trumpeting and holding the blue ribbon from which is suspended the Society's insignia, with the eagle grasping laurel leaves. A gilt husk inner border encloses this decoration and is framed on two sides by an underglaze blue butterfly and trellis "Fitzhugh" border. Around the base is a single cell border. The hare's head handles are finished in underglaze blue. The lid shows the insignia twice, enclosed in green wreaths, and also contains flower sprigs in *rouge de fer* and gilt. The outer border of the lid repeats the blue "Fitzhugh" pattern. OH: 4¾" (12.1 cm). OL: 7¼" (18.4 cm), OW: 4¾" (12.1 cm).

Plate XVIII. Two-handled cup and saucer, Ch'ien Lung, c. 1786–88, American market. The insignia of the Society of the Cincinnati is seen in two views: the obverse on the saucer and reverse on the cup. Also decorating the saucer is the gilt monogram "SS" of Samuel Shaw, the first secretary of this hereditary military society formed by officers of the Continental Line of the American Revolutionary army in 1783. Shaw served, as well, as the first American consul in China (1786–1794). These pieces are from a dinner service probably made in the early part of Shaw's term in China. OH (cup): 2⁹⁄₁₆″ (6.6 cm); Diam (saucer): 5⁹⁄₁₆″ (14.2 cm).

Plate XIX. Bowl and plate, Chia Ch'ing, c. 1810, American market. The fine sailing ship pictured here cannot be identified. It is not unlike those found on other ship pattern pieces of the period. The vessel is rendered in brown and *rouge de fer* with the riggings in *encre de chine*. The border is gilt. Diam (bowl): 4³⁄₁₆″ (10.7 cm); Diam (plate): 6¹⁄₁₆″ (15.4 cm).

Plate XX. Plate, Chia Ch'ing, c. 1800–1815, American
market. Distinctively American are those early nineteenth-
century porcelains which bear the eagle with trophies of
war. The service from which this plate comes was owned
by the Nichols family of Salem, Massachusetts. The spread-
winged eagle holds in its beak a banner reading "E
PLURIBUS UNUM." Diam: 9¹⁵⁄₁₆″ (25.3 cm).

XI. American Ship Designs

America's trading relationship with China began with the arrival of the *Empress of China* at Whampoa Anchorage in 1784. Major Samuel Shaw, the ship's supercargo or business agent, and Captain John Green were responsible for this historic first voyage which ended a year later with the delivery of a cargo, including six tons of export china, in New York, the home port. As noted previously, ware decorated with the insignia of the Society of the Cincinnati was commissioned at this time. Undoubtedly, porcelain bearing maritime designs, if not the flag of the new United States, was brought back for sale. Unfortunately, no known piece of export ware carries a representation of the *Empress of China*. If the decorators in Canton had been aware of the significance of this first contact between the newest and one of the most ancient societies, they surely would have vied for the honor of commemorating the event in porcelain.

Porcelain bearing ship portraits and other nautical symbols were then commonplace. Handsome bowls, plates, mugs or ship tankards, indeed whole services were produced for the European maritime nations during the 1700s. It has been written that "Every nation trading with China had portraits of its own ships done on porcelain. In fair or stormy weather, peacefully sailing, or in battle, the ships proudly adorn the porcelain of the time."[1] In addition to these specially commissioned works were those of a more crassly commercial nature; these were the souvenirs of the time, knick-knacks carried home by visiting sailors as mementoes of their trips away from home. By the time the Americans arrived in China, much of the originality and freshness of the nautical designs had been dissipated. What was left, however, was not to be sneered at—now, or then. Surviving examples of American ship porcelain are valued not only for their patriotic or sentimental value, but because the vast majority of them were executed with considerable skill and taste, if not always with accuracy.

The *Friendship* of Salem plate, figure 119, is one such fine piece. As noted in the caption to the illustration, this is an actual portrait of the vessel. Most ships pictured on American market pieces were copied from English engravings and/or were stock representations carried on hand by the Canton merchants and merely decorated with the proper flags and emblems. "The ship designs," it has been written, "very rarely portray any particular ship engaged in the trade with China. In most cases they resemble the more cumbersome vessels of prior centuries, and the main source for the decoration seems to have been printed patterns as used on business papers such as bills of lading."[2] A case in point is the portrait of the *Grand Turk* of Salem found on a handsome punch bowl now owned by the Peabody Museum. The *Grand Turk* was the first ship from Salem to sail to China in 1786. The design of the ship portrait, according to Carl L. Crossman, is probably an engraving of the British ship *Hall* which is used as the frontispiece to a work on naval architecture by William Hutchinson published in London in 1777.[3]

By the turn of the eighteenth century nearly thirty ships were sailing each year to the Orient. The amount of ship-decorated porcelain brought back to the States probably numbers in the many thousands. Although the art of decoration was definitely on the decline, the quality of the porcelain itself was—at least until the 1820s—fairly well maintained. The bowl and plate illustrated in color in these pages, plate XIX, is representative of the better ship porcelains of the early nineteenth century. It is perhaps too much to belabor the Chinese porcelain merchant for his practice of stocking ready-made patterns. As Homer Eaton Keyes, the former *Antiques* editor, has written, "they were but paralleling the habit of the potters of Staffordshire and Liverpool, who turned out great quantities of bowls and pitchers printed with transfer pictures of smart-looking vessels that needed but to be flagged and labeled at the purchaser's behest to become accepted portraits of pet craft."[4]

American ship porcelain pieces remain important—not as providing an accurate record of a trading era but rather as symbolic survivals of a romantic and historically-important period. At least we know from these imprecise renderings that the ships sailing to China in the early years were not the clipper ships of a later time, a misconception which refuses to die. Of the forms at all typical of ship-decorated ware, probably only the punch bowl with harbor scenes and the tankard or mug stand out as being important. Such a mug carrying the inscrutable inscription "Saturday Night" is illustrated here, figure 117. Among the delights of export ware, however, are those special exceptions to the general rules of form and decoration. Charles Ross's curious plate, figure 120, is just such an example. The story it tells, apocryphal or not, is the substance of engaging, colorful history.

NOTES

[1] Michel Beurdeley, *Chinese Trade Porcelain* (Rutland, Vermont: Charles E. Tuttle Co., 1962), p. 64.

[2] Homer Eaton Keyes, "Ship Designs," in *Chinese Export Porcelain*, ed. Elinor Gordon (New York: Universe Books, 1975), p. 38.

[3] Carl L. Crossman, *A Design Catalog of Chinese Export Porcelain* (Salem, Massachusetts: Peabody Museum, 1964), p. 11.

[4] Keyes, *ibid.*

Cylindrical mug, Ch'ien Lung, c. 1795, American market. The ship, in grisaille and *rouge de fer*, is flying two American flags and is sailing upon a sea of green enamel. Molded flowers at the handle terminals are decorated in *rouge de fer*. *See* also Gordon, pl. 1. OH: 4⅝₆″ (11 cm).

Plate, Chia Ch'ing, c. 1804, American market. This ship, flying two American flags and a blue banner, is painted in black and yellow with gilt; and the sea is in green enamel. The band border is of plain blue. The tureen of the service from which the plate comes carries the legend "America" on a ribbon beneath the ship. The vessel, owned by George Crowninshield of Salem, is known to have visited China in 1804, and it is possible that this service was acquired at that time. *See* Phillips, pl. 103. Diam: 9¾″ (24.8 cm).

117

118

119

Plate, Chia Ch'ing, c. 1820, American market. The central decoration, a sepia ship with riggings in *encre de chine*, is the "Friendship" of Salem, Massachusetts, and is an actual portrait of the vessel and not a copy of an English engraving as were most such Chinese representations. There were, however, several ships of this name and it is not certain which one is celebrated in this particular instance. The wide border contains four reserves of birds and flowers or Chinese figures in scenes, all executed in polychrome enamels. This type of border suggests a relatively late date of c. 1820 since it resembles those found on Rose Medallion and Mandarin export wares of the period. Hyde suggests the ship pictured was owned by the Silsbee family. The only other known plate of this sort is in the Peabody Museum, Salem. *See* Hyde, figs. 84 and 85. Diam: 9^{15}⁄$_{16}$" (25.2 cm).

120

Plate, Ch'ien Lung, c. 1790, American market. Although not decorated with the design of a ship, this piece belongs with those which have become a part of the legend of the seas. Family tradition has it that Charles Ross, a young man whose father was in partnership with Philadelphia merchant Robert Morris, sailed on one of the family ships to China. It was his duty to attend to the winding of the chronometer, an instrument for determining longitude at sea. Being of a forgetful nature, Ross overlooked this important duty. Later, in Canton, his shipmates presented him with this unique plate. The inscription is lettered in gilt. The plate was acquired from a descendent of the Ross family of Philadelphia. Diam: 9¾" (24.8 cm).

XII. American Family Services

This is the first book on export ware to adopt the phrase "American family" to cover a number of different types of decorated porcelain. It is more than a "catch-all" designed to sweep away all the loose ends which defy categorization. The majority of the pieces illustrated and discussed in this section are of the sort usually termed "pseudo-armorial." Some are just that, but others are worthy of a less pejorative term. More and more pieces of true American armorial ware are coming to light each year. In addition, we are continually gaining in knowledge concerning the genre-scenes which, in many cases, replaced the armorial motifs on custom-made familial tea sets and dinner services. All the porcelains discussed are, of course, of a late period—the last quarter of the eighteenth century until the 1830s or '40s. No attempt has been made here to document the innumerable Rose Medallion, Canton, Nanking, and Mandarin family services. These, for the most part, were produced *en masse*. Some early examples of such wares are surely deserving of attention, but it is impossible to study them with any hope of accuracy.

American family porcelain is sometimes simply identified by the presence of a monogram or cipher rather than a coat-of-arms. This is a serious and sad mistake. As has been pointed out earlier, the decoration of European armorial pieces gradually became simpler and simpler during the 1700s. A ciphered or monogrammed piece may be as English as it is American. Only when we can identify the person or family for whom the initials stand can we divide one nation from another. The only useful general rule to be followed is that Americans rarely used a coat-of-arms. This was especially true following the Revolutionary War, a period of obviously democratic tendencies.

There are, however, some true armorial services which have survived, albeit piecemeal, and these can be documented. The Elias Morgan tureen, figure 131, is one such object. Dated c. 1795, the tureen was undoubtedly ordered along with other parts of a dinner service and resembles those made in England at the time. Little is known about Morgan; he died at Killingsworthtown, near Milford, Connecticut, in 1813. A complete dinner set of armorial china was ordered by Philadelphia merchant Benjamin Fuller in 1787. Harrold E. Gillingham documented this story in an early issue of *Antiques*.[1] Unfortunately, only one piece, a badly damaged tray, has been found thousands of miles away in Ireland. Fuller's order, carried to China on the ship *Canton*, is known today, and this was accompanied by a sketch of the coat of arms. Specifically, Fuller instructed Captain Thomas Truxton as follows: "Inclos'd you have my Coat of Arms, which I request you to have put on every piece of China mentioned in the following List intended for Mrs. Fuller's own use—Small or large in proportion to the size of the Piece of China." What follows is a detailed list comprising some 200 pieces. Fuller must have been a particularly persnickety individual for he again repeated his instructions: "All this China (must be) of the most fashionable Kind and must have my Coat Armorial on each Piece—Small or large in proportion to the Size of the piece—The Best Nankeen China light Blue & White except the Coat of Arms which must be of the Colours there pictur'd—The Crest and Field to be a Silver Colour."

The Samuel Chase pudding dish, figure 126, is, as the caption notes, an enigma which has yet to be properly explained. The service carries not the Chase arms but those of Townley. Whether Chase inherited this from a Townley aunt or had it made in this manner is probably a question that will never be answered. It seems unlikely that a service of this size would have been brought by the family from England in c. 1736. Clare Le Corbeiller, who has given this service, a large part of which is now in the possession of the Metropolitan Museum of Art, more study than any other expert, concludes tentatively with the date 1785–90.[2]

The "pseudo-armorial" ciphered and monogrammed services are much more frequently encountered and easily explained. Typical of these wares are those of DeWitt Clinton, color plate XVI; Barry, figure 125; Derby, figure 139; Washington, figure 122; and the fine Adams service, figures 132–134. Less personally decorated objects are those which bear Masonic motifs such as the cider jug, figure 121, thought to have been ordered by John Brown of Providence, Rhode Island. An object adorned in this manner could have been as easily requested by an English customer with Masonic fraternal ties.

This leaves a wide variety of other motifs which are also general in nature but have been used primarily on American market pieces. Among these are such subjects as the New York and New Hampshire state arms, the Washington commemoratives, Mount Vernon, and Monticello. Export ware with various state arms have intrigued scholars of the decorative arts for many years. To see those of New York rendered in any sort of accurate fashion is, indeed, rare, and only in figure 127, a dish, has this end been attained. The tea caddy and coffeepot, figures 128 and 129, both display adaptations. This situation led Homer Eaton Keyes to conclude: "the employment of the New York arms as a decorative motive on Oriental porcelain represents a commercial experiment on the part of Chinese merchants rather than the fulfillment of some specific foreign order. Otherwise glaring discrepancies between original and copy would hardly have been tolerated."[3] In the same article Keyes also demolished a popularly-held belief that objects bearing the figure of Hope leaning on an anchor should or could be identified as carrying the Rhode Island arms. This motif, he found, could be associated with any number of times and places. The only other object unearthed by Keyes is one bearing the arms of Pennsylvania and dates from 1805. Since the time of this article (1930), however, the John A. Colby tea service with the arms of New Hampshire, figure 130, has come to light. In the Henry Francis du Pont Winterthur Museum Library is a bill showing that the 53 pieces were obtained through the merchant Yam Shinqua at Canton. An advertisement of his appeared in the Providence Gazette, May 12, 1804: "Yam Shinqua, China-Ware Merchant, at Canton, Begs Leave respectfully to inform the American Merchants, Supercargoes, and Captains, that he procures to be

Manufactured, in the Best Manner, all sorts of China-Ware with Arms, Cyphers, and other Decorations (if required) painted in a very superior style, and on the most reasonable Terms. All orders carefully and promptly attended to. Canton. Jan. 8, 1804."[4]

Of the other objects illustrated in this section, several more are of particular interest. Mount Vernon scenes, figure 137, are rare but well-known; those of Monticello, figure 138, are just being studied. The Washington memorial pieces are from one of two known dinner services, figures 135 and 136. A sepia and gold-decorated mug, also in our collection, contains the same memorial monument but has no cipher and is decorated with an entirely different border motif. It is most likely that the Chinese merchants found a ready market for such mourning art following the death of Washington in 1799, and had produced many more items than those accounted for in the two services.

Three pieces dating from the mid-1800s, figures 143–145, are included here to illustrate decorative motifs which are sometimes considered to be of an earlier vintage. They are in no sense inferior wares, but neither should they be considered exceptional. They are simply typical of motifs popular in domestic ware of the period.

The final illustration, figure 146, is of a very handsome cream pot made for the Mexican market. The history of export porcelain destined for Spanish and Portuguese-speaking areas of the Americas is closely linked with the Iberian peninsula as is that of North America with England. Students of export ware would be well advised to explore this interesting chapter.[5]

NOTES

[1] Harrold E. Gillingham, "A Lost Set of Eighteenth-Century Oriental Lowestoft," *Chinese Export Porcelain*, ed. Elinor Gordon (New York: Universe Books, 1975), pp. 140–41.

[2] Clare Le Corbeiller, *China Trade Porcelain: Patterns of Exchange* (New York: The Metropolitan Museum of Art, 1974), pp. 61–63.

[3] Homer Eaton Keyes, "'State Arms on Chinese Lowestoft," Chinese Export Porcelain, ed. Elinor Gordon (New York: Universe Books, 1975), p. 124.

[4] Arlene M. Palmer, *A Winterthur Guide to Chinese Export Porcelain* (New York: Crown Publishers, Inc., 1976), p. 124.

[5] *See* S. S. Mottahedeh, "Numismatic Sources of Chinese Export Porcelain Decoration," *Connoisseur* (October, 1969). pp. 115–16.

121

Cider jug, Ch'ien Lung, c. 1790, American or English market. Although armorial in basic form, the "societal" china made in the late eighteenth century, much of it for the American market, does not follow the rules of heraldic decoration. Only the monogram "JB" marks this piece as belonging to a particular individual or family. The initials may be those of John Brown (1736–1803), a prominent Providence, Rhode Island, merchant active in the China trade. Chinese export ware was occasionally decorated with Masonic symbols, including Solomon's seal, the sun and moon, calipers, compasses, plumbline, trowel, etc. One tea set is known to have the United States arms framed by the calipers and square. The symbols on this jug are rendered in polychrome enamels, sepia, and gilt. OH: 9″ (22.9 cm).

Mug, Ch'ien Lung, c. 1790, American market. Unmistakably American is the mug which carries the simple monogram "GW" for George Washington. The decoration is armorial, but is not heavily weighted with heraldic elements. An ermine-lined blue mantle surrounds the shield. The border is a blue enamel wavy band with polychrome floral sprigs. A large punch bowl with an identical monogrammed shield draped by an ermine-lined mantle belonged to George Washington and may be seen at Mount Vernon. OH: 6¹⁄₁₆″ (16.8 cm).

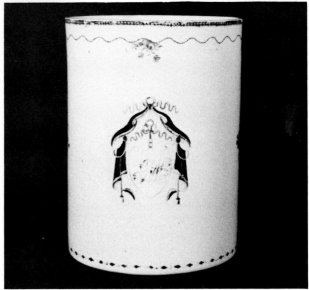

122

Plate, Ch'ien Lung, c. 1790, American market. The service from which this plate comes was owned by Charles Washington (1738–1799), youngest brother of George Washington. Two plates from the service were presented to the Mount Vernon Ladies' Association by a descendant of the family. The flowers are rendered in polychrome enamels and *rouge de fer* with insects in sepia. The use of these creatures in the decoration is a most unusual touch. Diam: 6⅜" (16.2 cm).

124

Cup and saucer, Ch'ien Lung, c. 1790, American market. This cup and saucer were part of a tea service brought to Philadelphia by Captain John Barry (1745–1803), Revolutionary War naval officer, for his second wife, Sarah Austin. They were married on July 7, 1777. Floral festoons of polychrome enamels surround the shield with the monogram "SB" and form the outer border. OH (cup): 2½" (6.4 cm); Diam (saucer): 5¾" (13.7 cm).

123

125

Covered urn, Ch'ien Lung, c. 1795, American
market. The Barry family of Philadelphia also
owned a garniture set with a similar design
motif. John Barry was responsible for bringing
a number of important porcelain pieces from China
to Philadelphia. Two oval panels contain classical
landscapes in sepia. The borders are in blue enamel
and gilt. OH: 11⅛" (28.2 cm), OW: 4⅜" (11.1
cm).

Pudding dish, Ch'ien Lung, c. 1790, American market. The Samuel Chase service is one of the most curious examples of armorial ware known to have existed in America. The Metropolitan Museum of Art owns 248 pieces from this service, and each carries, as does the pudding dish, the arms of Margaret Townley, the wife of a Chase uncle. That Samuel Chase (1741–1811) of Annapolis, Maryland, used the Townley arms is substantiated by his armorial bookplate now in the possession of the Library of Congress. It is possible that he inherited the service and then adopted the arms for other uses. On the other hand, it is possible that Chase, a signer of the Declaration of Independence and justice of the United States Supreme Court, ordered the service himself from China. The Townley arms are rendered in polychrome enamels, *rouge de fer*, and black. Polychrome enamel floral sprigs decorate the edge and are enclosed by gilt borders. Diam: 5⅞″ (14.9 cm), OH: 2⅛″ (5.4 cm).

126

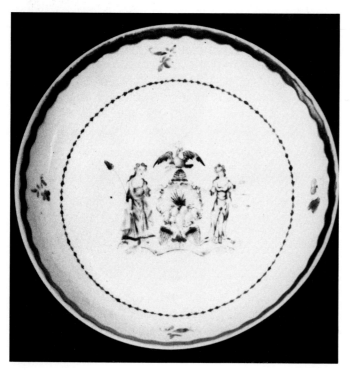

127

Dish, Ch'ien Lung, c. 1790, American market. The design is of the arms of New York State, which were adopted in 1778. In the official version, Liberty and Justice stand on a scroll bearing the word "Excelsior," and hold between them a cartouche displaying the sun rising over a group of mountains. The shield is surmounted by a half-globe upon which is perched an eagle. The use of the full arms on this dish is rare. They are painted in polychrome enamels, black, and gilt; the borders are in blue enamel and gilt. Diam: 5½″ (14 cm).

129

128

Tea caddy, Ch'ien Lung, c. 1790, American market. The arms of New York State have been adapted on this object. The figures are drawn in the Chinese style in a charming if not primitive manner. Polychrome enamel colors and gilt are used in the arms, and the eagle is rendered in black. The borders are in blue enamel and gilt. OH (with cover): 5½″ (13 cm).

Coffeepot, Ch'ien Lung, c. 1790, American market. The figures found on this object are more finely drawn than most found in similar New York State designs. The manner in which the arms have been adapted differs somewhat from that found on other pieces. A cipher, "EF" for Eliza Fisher, has been worked into the shield. This adaptation differs in other ways as well: Liberty is seated rather than standing; the eagle's wings are spread upward instead of downward; and two small shields have not been used. The arms are decorated in sepia and *rouge de fer*, the banner in rose, and the globe in black enamel. Border and trim are in gilt. OH: 9½″ (24.2 cm).

Dish, Chia Ch'ing, c. 1800–1810, American market. The arms of New Hampshire are found on this piece. The unique tea service from which it was taken was made for John A. Colby of Concord, New Hampshire. In a circle within a blue and gilt oval, the arms show a sun setting to the right of a ship without a mast riding on a sea of green. Above is the monogram "JAC". The border is executed in blue and gilt. Diam: 6½" (16.5 cm).

130

Covered tureen, Ch'ien Lung, c. 1790–95, American market. The arms of Elias Morgan of Guilford, Connecticut, are painted on this true armorial piece. A gilt shield is emblazoned with a green rampant lion and is enclosed in a shield of blue enamel. A crossed wreath of wheat in green enamel, black, and gilt surrounds the shield. The outer blue enamel border has a continuous gilt decoration. There are only two other known American services with coats of arms. Diam (top): 10⅞" (27.6 cm), OW: 8" (20.3 cm), OH (with cover): 7¾" (19.7 cm).

131

Teapot, Chia Ch'ing, c. 1800, American market. This piece is from a tea set made for Mehitable Adams (1760–1824), a member of the distinguished Braintree, Massachusetts, family. In 1760 she married Joseph Neale Arnold. The cipher "MA" is painted in gilt. The hearts are rendered in *rouge de fer* with green and blue enamel colors and gilt. The borders are in blue enamel with gilt stars. This, and other objects made for Mehitable Adams, were purchased from a direct descendant of the family. OH: 4½" (11.4 cm).

Sugar bowl, Chia Ch'ing, c. 1800, American market. The sugar bowl from the Adams set is a handsomely proportioned piece and is decorated with applied leaves on each side. Diam (top): 4⅛" (10.5 cm), OH: (10.2 cm).

134

Cream pot, Chia Ch'ing, c. 1800, American market. This object is fashioned with the same care and simple lines as the other pieces of the Adams set. OH: 4¾" (10.5 cm).

135

Tureen, Chia Ch'ing, c. 1800, American market. The Chinese were adept at producing memorial procelains in proper mourning-art style. This is a piece from one of three known dinner services with the Washington funerary monument and the same border of drapery and floral sprays. These sets must have been ordered shortly after George Washington died on December 14, 1799. The script monogram "JRL" in an oval reserve is sometimes said to belong to John R. Latimer of Philadelphia, but it is more likely that this set was made for Judith and Robert Lewis, a nephew of Washington. A second mourning set of china has the monogram "PAS," and the third set contains no monogram. All the decoration is in a somber scheme of sepia, dark brown, and gilt. Around the rim is a band of leaves between rows of gilt stars. A platter from this service with a reticulated border is in the White House collection. OH: 4⅜" (11.2 cm), OL: 6⁷⁄₁₆" (17.4 cm).

144

136

Platter, Chia Ch'ing, c. 1800, American market. Part of the same "JRL" set is this Washington memorial platter. OL: 11" (27.9 cm), OW: 7⅞" (20 cm).

137

Butter tub with underplate, Chia Ch'ing, c.
1805–15, American market. This vignette of
Mount Vernon appears on other pieces of export
ware and is accompanied with a variety of
borders. Recent research indicates that the
scene may have been copied from a painting
now hanging in the director's office at Mount
Vernon. Duplicates of painting of this sort were
often taken to China and copied by a decorator.
The view is drawn in sepia, red-brown, and
gilt. The border is known as a swag and tassel.
OH (tub): 2¾" (7 cm); Underplate: 6¹⁵⁄₁₆"
(17.6 cm) x 5⅛" (13 cm).

138

Soup dish, Chia Ch'ing, c. 1820, American market. Although not as historically important as the Mount Vernon pieces and those associated with Washington, those identified with Monticello and Jefferson are rare and intriguing to the collector. Why this decoration was used will remain a mystery, although it is possible that friends of Jefferson or members of his family did order such a specially decorated service. The oval sepia vignette shows the homes and grounds of Monticello and a man with a wheelbarrow in the foreground. The sawtooth inner- and leaf scroll outer-borders are painted in brown and gilt. Diam: 9¾″ (24.8 cm).

139

Plate, Ch'ien Lung, c. 1786, American market. Elias Hasket
Derby (1739–1799) ordered a 171-piece dinner service in
1786 and the next year it was brought to Salem, Massachusetts, on the first New England ship to reach Canton,
the "Grand Turk." This was one of many ships which
were financed by Derby and were to establish his fortune
as a great merchant prince. This immense service was not
the only one to be delivered on the "Grand Turk"; a tea
service of 101 pieces, similarly decorated, was also specially
made. The decoration on this plate—crest in rose and
black enamel colors with gilt, figure in sepia, motto reading "Spero," and "EHD" cipher in *rouge de fer* and gilt—
is that used on both the dinner and the tea set. Diam:
9¼" (23.5 cm).

Saucer, Chia Ch'ing, c. 1815, American market. The set to which this saucer belongs is thought to have been owned by a member of a prominent Philadelphia family, perhaps a Chew. It is decorated with a wide leaf scroll band in dark brown on a tan ground, and has highlights in gilt. Diam: 6¾₁₆″ (15.7 cm).

141

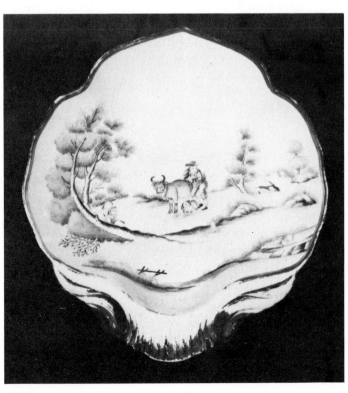

Shrimp dish, Chia Ch'ing, c. 1805, American market. This quaint pastoral design is thought to have originated with Mary Hollingsworth Morris, a Philadelphia Quaker who had made a sketch of a scene on her father's farm. Her brother, Henry, engaged in the China trade, took her pattern to Canton in the early 1800s. He ordered two dinner sets with this decoration done in black and trimmed with gilt. Mary and her husband, Isaac Morris, considered the gilt trim to be too ostentatious for their Quaker taste. The set was returned to Henry and a new service ordered with the same decoration in sepia. Other Philadelphians, among them the Pembertons, found the pattern to their taste and ordered additional sets in both black and sepia. This shrimp dish is from the original set. In 1962 a 55-piece tea set with the same design was recovered from the remains of a ship sunk in Delaware Bay in the early nineteenth century. OH: 10″ (25.4 cm), OW: 9¼″ (23.5 cm).

140

142

Pierced and interwoven basket, Ch'ia Ching,
1800–1820, American market. This piece
comes from a service made for the marriage
of Samuel Cabot and Eliza Perkins, daughter
of Thomas Handasyd Perkins, a well-known
Boston merchant in the China trade. It is
thought to be a unique service in terms of
decoration; the form is copied from a Wedg-
wood prototype. "Fitzhugh" four-panel decoration in blue is used with a pagoda rather
than with the usual central medallion. The
unusual motif is believed to be patterned
after the pagoda on the island of Honan.
See Crossman, pgs. 27–28.

Small plate, Tao Kuang, c. 1840, American
market. The "Cabbage Leaf" pattern is one
of those which gained in popularity in
North America as the nineteenth century
advanced. Green leaves radiate from a gold
Chinese symbol, and butterflies in yellow,
blue, black, and red enamel colors rest at
the inner rim. Diam: 6¾" (17.1 cm).

143

144

Plate, Tao Kuang, c. 1840–50, American market. Columbia, dressed in rose, yellow, turquoise, and *rouge de fer*, is shown with a sword, American shield, and brown eagle. Polychrome enamel colors are used in scattered floral sprigs and a floral band border. Diam: 10″ (25.4 cm).

Sugar bowl, 1840–1875, American market. For this decoration the Chinese relied primarily on A. B. Durand's etching of 1823 after the famous painting "The Declaration of Independence," by John Trumbull. The Canton enamelers seem to have taken certain liberties with the original since the periwigged eighteenth-century statesmen look remarkably like nineteenth-century bald-headed Chinese. A spread eagle similar to the type used on many "Fitzhugh" patterned pieces has been substituted for the trophies of war found in Durand's etching. The spread eagle is in sepia, and the shield is, of course, red, white, and blue. The banner is painted in rose, and all the signers are executed in polychrome enamel colors. Although the general shapes of forms with the Declaration of Independence design were popular in the late eighteenth century, details on this piece, such as the handles, are so carelessly modeled as to reinforce the late date assigned to it. OH: 4⁵⁄₁₆″ (11 cm), OW: 4⅞″ (12.4 cm).

145

Cream pot, Ch'ien Lung, c. 1790, Mexican market. A number of Chinese export porcelain services were decorated for this market using proclamation medals struck after Charles IV acceded to the Spanish throne in 1788. The decoration is taken from a medal by Geronimo Antonio Gil (rendered CIL by the Chinese decorator), Chief Engraver of the Mint of Mexico during the last quarter of the eighteenth century. The design is of the arms of the Consulate of Mexico and are executed in polychrome enamel colors with sepia, *encre de chine*, and gilt. The shield containing the arms is flanked by the figure of Mercury, god of trade, and a Spanish frigate of war. Export wares made for Mexico and other Latin American countries rarely have made their way to North America and Europe in recent years. OH: 3⅞″ (9.8 cm).

146

XIII. American Eagle Designs

No form of export ware is more likely to excite the interest of the American collector than that decorated with the national emblem of the eagle. Considering the extreme value of such porcelain, connoisseurs of antique ceramics, wherever they may dwell, would be wise to keep on the lookout for the ubiquitous bird. It was not a creature favored by that most American of eighteenth-century statesmen, Benjamin Franklin (he urged the use of the wild turkey as the American symbol), but since his time it has achieved a popularity approaching fanaticism. Perhaps only in Prussia and in imperial Russia, has this stately bird, in double form, been as popular an icon. As mentioned in the Introduction, modern decorators or "clobberers" have been ineluctably attracted to this most valuable of species.

The first American eagle to appear on export ware was, in the words of Homer Eaton Keyes, "a rather sorry looking bird, far more closely resembling an English sparrow than the fowl of freedom."[1] It is to Keyes, an extraordinarily felicitous writer and indefatigable researcher, that we owe most of our knowledge about the eagle on Chinese porcelain. Since this ware is but a very minor part of the total story of porcelain production and one that occurred at a very late date, European scholars have uniformly ignored its existence. Curators in American institutions, for the most part, have merely repeated Keyes's words written forty-seven years ago. This writer has found that they are on safe ground doing so, but, clearly, a new, thorough study of this design motif—how it was presented to the Chinese and used by them—is badly needed. Keyes's "sparrow" is deserving of much more attention.

It is not difficult to see why Keyes chose to describe the first renderings of the eagle in such terms. The creature seen on the sugar bowl and helmet creamer, figure 148, is, indeed, a droopy bird. Keyes has outlined three variations on this particular early theme, differences which center on the decoration of the shield. Two of these are illustrated in figure 148: a red striped shield, and one that is decorated with a simple floral sprig. A third variation contains a monogram or cipher. Pieces decorated with this form of eagle are surely the earliest of such ware. The source for the rendering of the bird is difficult to pinpoint. Keyes suggests that Massachusetts coins of 1787–88 or such printed sources as letterheads and official government papers may have provided the decorators with their guidelines. So far none of the possible sources pinpointed by experts, however, contain all of the various design elements.

Some writers have stated that eagle-decorated china was custom-made. The presence of several versions of at least the "sparrow" type suggest, however, that this was not the case. It is most probable that decorated sets were kept on hand and that only the shield area was left free for elaboration. This section of the design, of course, was that perfectly suited for pseudo-armorial decoration.

Sometime early in the nineteenth century a true version of the eagle used on the Great Seal of the United States did appear. This was to be copied many thousands of times. Along with it emerged two other versions: with extended or spread wings (figure 149, color plate XX), or in uplifted flight, figure 147. Use of the "Fitzhugh" border, the eagle replacing the customary central medallion, was to become common practice. Porcelain of this sort was not to be shipped to America in the vast quantities ascribed to simpler Canton, Nanking, Rose Medallion, and Mandarin wares of the nineteenth century, but as Keyes stated in 1930, "Judging by the frequency with which specimens appear in salesroom and shop today, it must so far have fulfilled expectations as to be imported in large quantities, ordinarily in the form of tea services, and of individual pieces, such as tall mugs and vases."[2] Since 1930, of course, the market has considerably narrowed. This is especially true of the very fine pieces, obviously custom-made, such as those which comprise the Nichols family service, color plate XX.

NOTES

[1] Homer Eaton Keyes, "American Eagle Lowestoft," *Chinese Export Porcelain*, ed. Elinor Gordon (New York: Universe Books, 1975), p. 120.
 [2] *Ibid.*

147   Lighthouse coffeepot, Chia Ch'ing, c. 1800, American market. An eagle in flight is carrying the message "IN GOD WE HOPE" on a rose banner held in its beak. In his talons is a gilt trumpet of fame. The eagle is executed in sepia. The major portion of the other pieces in this service are to be found at the Henry Francis du Pont Winterthur Museum. OH: 9¹³⁄₁₆" (25 cm), OW (spout to handle): 9⅝" (24.5 cm).

148

Left, sugar bowl, *right,* helmet cream pitcher, Chia Ch'ing, c. 1800, American market. A "sparrow"-type eagle is painted on both pieces in sepia and gilt. The shield used on the pitcher carries red stripes and the top border is a brown band with gilt stars. The shield painted on the sugar bowl contains a gilt floral sprig. The pitcher derives its unusual name from the form it assumes when it is turned upside down —that of a helmet. Held stable in this position by a handle that can be hooked over a surface's edge, it can be used as a candleholder. The base is formed with an indentation suitable for holding a candle. OH (helmet pitcher): 5⅜" (13.7 cm), OW: 6½" (16.5 cm); OH (sugar bowl): 5½" (14 cm), OW: 5¾" (14.6 cm).

Leaf-shaped dish, Chia Ch'ing, c. 1800-1815, American market. The usual central "Fitzhugh" medallion has been replaced with an eagle in sepia bearing a shield with the initials "JLH" painted in gold. The banner and motto, "E Pluribus Unum," are executed in puce. The butterfly and trellis border is decorated in a green enamel. OW: 6" (15.2 cm), OL: 7¾" (19.7 cm).

149

Tea bowl and saucer, Chia Ch'ing, c. 1810, American market. This version of the eagle design is identical to that first used as an adaptation of the Great Seal of the United States and on the 1807 American half-dollar. The dark brown and gilt eagle bears a shield on its breast with the monogram "HLH." It is grasping a leafless laurel branch and an arrow in its talons. The grape and vine outer border is executed in two shades of gilt. Diam (tea bowl): 3⁷⁄₁₆" (8.7 cm), OH: 1¾" (4.5 cm); Diam (saucer): 5½" (14 cm).

150

Selected Bibliography

The following works are referred to in the illustration captions:

Beurdeley, Michel. *Chinese Trade Porcelain*. Rutland, Vt., and London, 1962.

Cox, Warren E. *The Book of Pottery and Porcelain*. New York, 1963.

Crossman, Carl L. *A Design Catalog of Chinese Export Porcelain for the American Market 1785 to 1840*. Salem, Mass., Peabody Museum, 1964.

An Exhibition of China Trade Porcelain. New Haven, Conn., 1968.

Gordon, Elinor, ed. *Chinese Export Porcelain*. New York, 1975.

Howard, David Sanctuary. *Chinese Armorial Porcelain*. London, 1974.

Hyde, J. A. Lloyd. *Oriental Lowestoft*, 3rd edition. Newport, England, 1964.

Le Corbeiller, Clare. *China Trade Porcelain: Patterns of Exchange*, Additions to the Helena Woolworth McCann Collection in the Metropolitan Museum of Art. New York, 1974.

Mount Vernon China. Mount Vernon, Va., 1962.

Mudge, Jean McClure. *Chinese Export Porcelain for the American Trade 1785-1835*. Newark, Del., 1962.

Palmer, Arlene M. *A Winterthur Guide to Chinese Export Porcelain*. New York, 1976.

Phillips, John Goldsmith. *China Trade Porcelain*. Cambridge, Mass., 1956.

The Reeves Collection of Chinese Export Porcelain. Lexington, Va.

Roth, Stig. *Chinese Porcelain Imported by the Swedish East India Company*, translated by Mary G. Clarke. Gothenburg, Sweden, 1965.

Scheurleer, D. F. Lunsingh. *Chinese Export Porcelain: Chine de Commande*. New York and London, 1974.

Tudor-Craig, Sir Algernon. *Armorial Porcelain of the Eighteenth Century*. London, 1925.

Williamson, George C. *The Book of Famille Rose*, 1927, reprint by Charles E. Tuttle, Rutland, Vt., 1970.

In addition to the above works, the reader will find the following titles of assistance and interest:

Chinese Export Porcelain and Enamels. Wilmington, Del., 1957.

Donnelly, Blanc de Chine, *The Porcelain of Te-Hua in Fukien*, London and New York, 1969.

Hobson, R. L. *Chinese Pottery and Porcelain: An Account of the Potter's Art in China from Primitive Times to the Present Day*. vol. II (Ming and Ch'ing Porcelain). London, 1915.

Honey, William Bowyer. *The Ceramic Art of China and Other Countries of the Far East*. London, 1945.

Jenyns, Soames. *Later Chinese Porcelain: The Ch'ing Dynasty* (1644-1912). London, 1951.

Le Corbeiller, Clare. *China Trade Porcelain: A Study in Double Reflections*. New York, 1973.

Quincy, Josiah. *The Journals of Major Samuel Shaw, the First Consul at Canton*. Boston, 1847.

Index